The Penguin Atlas of
HUMAN SEXUAL BEHAVIOR

"Sexual and reproductive health is an intrinsic and essential component of general health for both women and men. Moreover, it is a prerequisite for the health of infants and children, for adolescents and for people beyond reproductive years. By extension, it is a vital part of the health of families and communities upon which human development rests. Dr Mackay's atlas highlights many features of this important health dimension in an educational and creative fashion."

> — Dr Gro Harlem Brundtland MD, MPH
> Director-General
> World Health Organization

"Now that we have entered the age of economic globalization, it is becoming increasingly important for sexologists and other health professionals to take a global view of sexual health as well. Professor Mackay's atlas represents another pioneering step in this direction. In compact form, it provides a great deal of basic information that is otherwise difficult to find, even for professionals. However, here not only the specialist, but also the lay public can gain quick insights into a variety of sexual issues and develop an awareness of our common humanity, even in the realm of the sexual. The book will undoubtedly prove very useful for teachers at every academic level, to students in a number of fields, to journalists, and to public officials. This atlas needed to be written, and one can only congratulate Professor Mackay for having taken the initiative."

> — Professor Erwin J. Haeberle, PhD
> Director, Archive of Sexology
> Robert Koch Institute, Berlin

"*The Penguin Atlas of Human Sexual Behavior* is an innovative way of presenting many issues of sexology in lively, creative format."

> — Professor Eli Coleman, PhD
> President, 1997-2001
> World Association of Sexology

Also in this series:

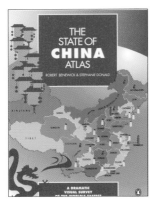

THE STATE OF CHINA ATLAS
by Robert Benewick and Stephanie Donald

THE STATE OF THE WORLD ATLAS
sixth edition
by Dan Smith

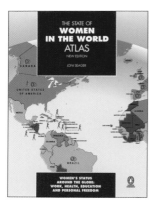

THE STATE OF WOMEN IN THE WORLD ATLAS
second edition
by Joni Seager

The Penguin Atlas of
HUMAN SEXUAL BEHAVIOR

Judith Mackay

PENGUIN
REFERENCE

PENGUIN REFERENCE

Published by the Penguin Group
Penguin Putnam Inc., 375 Hudson Street,
New York, New York 10014, USA
Penguin Books Ltd., 27 Wrights Lane,
London W8 5TZ, England
Penguin Books Australia Ltd., Ringwood,
Victoria, Australia
Penguin Books Canada Ltd., 10 Alcorn Avenue,
Toronto, Ontario, Canada M4V 3B2
Penguin Books (NZ) Ltd., 182-190 Wairau Road,
Auckland 10, New Zealand

First published in Penguin Reference 2000
10 9 8 7 6 5 4 3 2 1

Penguin Reference paperback 0 14 05.1479 1

Produced for the Penguin Group by
Myriad Editions Limited
53 Old Steine, Brighton BN1 1NH, UK
myriad@dircon.co.uk
www.myriadeditions.com

Edited and co-ordinated for Myriad Editions
by Candida Lacey
with Jannet King
Design by Corinne Pearlman
with thanks to Erica Smith and Carol Seatory
Maps created by Isabelle Lewis

Printed and bound in China
Produced by Phoenix Offset Limited
under the supervision of
The Hanway Press, London

CONTENTS

CONTENTS

INTRODUCTION

"When people are fed and clothed, then they think about sex."

— K'ung Fu-Tzu (Confucius)
551-479 BC

The human body is a sexed body — physically, mentally, psychologically, hormonally. While most adults know enough about sex for practical purposes, many are not aware of how this most universal experience comes complete with an array of cultural and international similarities and differences; and how this essentially private activity often raises public issues.

This atlas arose from discussions with the late Anne Benewick, then Managing Director of Myriad. As a physician, living in Hong Kong since 1967, I had moved from curative, hospital-based medicine to preventive health in 1984. I was telling Anne how I lobbied for maternity leave, initiated a rape crisis hotline, and opened the first refuge for battered women in Asia. I campaigned, lectured, and encouraged men and women to understand their bodies and how they worked, and to participate in health-care decisions. Twenty years ago sex was never discussed in public in Asia, but when I started broadcasting and writing articles on sexual issues, there was overwhelming public support. On call-in radio programs, people wept with gratitude to find that they were not alone with their problems.

Whilst there were many books on sex, none collated data across the range of sex issues — from the intensely personal to the economic and political. We wanted to write a book for everyone, not just for those in the field of health and reproduction, sexology, gender studies, anthropology, crime, law, religion, and history; but also for young people and adults who wanted to learn more about sex for themselves.

The task was not easy. There is no central global depository for sex information, very few sexology institutes or specialists, and only a handful of countries with comprehensive statistics. Sex research, where it exists, is usually fertility-related, rather than sex-orientated. Even definitions vary, e.g. of sex counseling, obscenity, or "normal sex." The key concept of "normal sex" in this atlas is sex with "informed consent." This therefore excludes pedophilia as a child cannot give informed consent. It also excludes rape and other crimes of violence, and bestiality and necrophilia, as neither beast nor dead body can "consent."

Attitudes towards sex and sexuality are constantly challenged and levels of tolerance never permanent. We have included a range of key indicators, including laws and attitudes towards homosexuality, availability of sex education, rates of marriage, divorce, and adultery, and degrees of state censorship. The atlas begins with the origins of sexual reproduction millions of years ago, and why we have sex at all. It moves to sex practices and issues of today and ends by speculating where sex will go in the future: sex is already in cyberspace and is sure to take place in real space in the first lunar colony.

Many people have helped in the preparation of this atlas. Firstly, my thanks to all those at United Nations' organizations: at UNAIDS (Joint United Nations Program on HIV/AIDS), James Sherry, Michel Elie Xavier J. Carael, Roeland Monaschm, and Bernhard Schwartlander; at UNCJIN (UN Criminal Justice Information Network), Adam C. Bouloukos; at UNICEF (United Nations Children's Fund), Warren Feek, now Director of The Communication Initiative; at UNFPA (United Nations Population Fund), Stephen Flaetgen; at The World Bank, Prabhat Jha, now Economics Advisory Service, WHO; at WHO (World Health Organization), Paul Bloem, Stella Elliot Efua Dorkenoo, Jane Ferguson, Ahmet M. Gulmezoglu, Paul Van Look, C. Garcia Moreno, Derek Yach, and Soon-Young Yoon.

My particular thanks go to: Erwin Haeberle, Director, Archive of Sexology, Robert Koch Institute, Berlin, Germany, author of *The Sex Atlas* and co-author of *Sexual Behavior in Modern China*, for his invaluable website, database and advice; Sunetra Puri, International Planned Parenthood Federation (IPPF); Nigel Warner, International Lesbian and Gay Association (ILGA); Virginia Wenzel and Catherine Baber, Amnesty International; Kate Young, Womankind Worldwide, England; Lam Tai-hing, University of Hong Kong; Demographic and Health Survey (DHS) program staff, Macro International, USA and South Africa; Liana Zhou and Jennifer Corbin, Kinsey Institute, University of Indiana, USA; Irene Grignac, International Union for the Scientific Study of Population (IUSSP).

For their advice on particular subjects, I would like to thank:

The Sex Drive Richard Mackay, Environmental Officer, University of Cambridge, UK;

Homosexuality Jeff Walsh, !OutProud!, The National Coalition for Gay, Lesbian, Bisexual and Transgender Youth and *Oasis Magazine*; Milton Diamond, University of Hawaii, USA; Donald J. West, Institute of Criminology, University of Cambridge, UK; Simon Chapman, Department of Public Health and Community Medicine, University of Sydney, Australia;

Transgender Zoe-Jane Playdon, South Thames Department of Postgraduate Medical and Dental Education, University of London, UK;

Sex Appeal Devendra Singh, University of Texas, USA; Linda Mealey, College of St. Benedict, St. Joseph, USA;

Dating Ann Sturley, AIDS Project at the East-West Center, Honolulu, Hawaii, USA; Diane Kholos Wysocki, University of Nebraska at Kearney, USA;

Choose Your Partner David Buss, University of Texas, USA;

Marriage Ripley Forbes, Department of Health and Human Services, USA;

Contraception Mitchell Warren, Population Services International, Europe; Carolyn J. Ross, Population Action International, Washington, DC, USA; Penny Kane and Pamela McGrath, Family Planning Australia Inc.;

Pregnancy Nina J. Pane Pinto, International Programs Center, US Bureau of the Census;

Sex Education Philippa Hanscombe, BBC World Service, UK; Trish Hogg, Open University, UK;

Safer Sex Clive Kitchener and Simon White, Durex Condoms, London International Group plc.; Carlo Nuss and Andrew Plumer, POPLINE and Population Reports, Johns Hopkins University School of Public Health, USA;

Sexually-Transmitted Infections Michel Hubert, Facultés universitaires Saint-Louis, Brussels;

Counseling Edward O. Laumann, Department of Sociology, University of Chicago, USA; Marj Thoburn, Head of Psychosexual Therapy, Relate Marriage Guidance, UK; Nia Pryde, psychosexual counselor, Hong Kong;

The Economics of Sex Patrick Dixon, Director Global Change Ltd., UK; Ken Warner, University of Michigan, USA;

Female Genital Excision Jeri T. Smith, Research, Action and Information Network for Bodily Integrity of Women, USA; Fran P. Hosken, Women's International Network News, USA;

Circumcision Tim Hammond, National Organisation to Halt the Abuse and Routine Mutilation of Males (NOHARMM); J.P. Warren, physician, UK;

Harassment Evonne Von Heussen-Countryman, National Anti-Stalking and Harassment Support Association (NASH), UK;

The Future of Sex Trudy Barber, author on cybersex, fetishism, and transgressive sexuality, UK; Ian Pearson, futurologist and author of *The Macmillan Atlas of the Future*;

Aphrodisiacs Judy Mills, TRAFFIC, c/o World Wildlife Fund, Hong Kong.

I owe a special debt to my husband John, for his support and contributions throughout the entire gestational period of the atlas. Also, to my two researchers who located data and came up with many creative ideas: Kate Allen, now University of Cambridge Local Examinations Syndicate, UK, and Judi Supplee, internet researcher extraordinaire.

Finally, my thanks to all the wonderful colleagues and friends at Myriad Editions for their diverse talents and their individual and collective contribution: Candida Lacey, Corinne Pearlman, Jannet King, Isabelle Lewis, Bob Benewick, and never forgetting Anne Benewick.

Judith Mackay
Hong Kong
February 14, 2000

THE SEX DRIVE

"The problem of why sex exists, and in particular of why the vast inefficiency of maleness exists, seems to me biology's greatest, most exciting problem." – William D. Hamilton, 1999

year 2000
2–4.5 million years ago
28 million years ago
300 million years ago
400 million years ago
600 million years ago
2,000 million years ago
3,000 million years ago
4,300 million years ago

GENES

• Charles Darwin noted that sex provides a method of selective breeding, complementary to natural selection by the external environment.

• Richard Dawkins has proposed that animals and plants are the throwaway vehicles of "selfish genes." Our selection of a partner and sex practices are driven by genes in order for them to replicate as successfully as possible. Each time we use contraception we fight our genes.

• Genes survive by the birth of a sibling as well as by offspring. We value relatives roughly in proportion to the similarity of their genes to ours.

Some childless aunts, aphids, wasps, bees, naked mole rats, and Caribbean snapping shrimps abandon procreation and invest their energies into helping relatives' genes survival.

• Young children are up to 60 times more likely to be killed by a step parent — almost always a stepfather — than by a natural parent. However, some scientists argue that adoption gives adoptive parents the opportunity to pass on their cultural imprinting. Sex and inheritance is an interaction between genes, brains, environmental events, and cultural influences learned and handed down from generation to generation.

• Genes are losing their privileged position as the carriers of biological information. Technology enables us to control and change genes; biological information can also be stored on computers. Genes will become just one of the many means of manipulating the world.

• Sex is increasingly removed from human reproduction — with contraception, test-tube babies, surrogate parenthood, cloning, and virtual reality sex.

• At least 450 species of birds and mammals engage in same-sex activity, which is difficult to explain by the selfish gene theory alone.

SOCIAL CONDUCT

• Males must compete to impregnate, while all fertile females are virtually assured of finding a mate. This is why males are mostly larger and, in animal species, more colorful.

• Sex is commonest between high-ranking males and females of all ranks. "Superior" male plants may fertilize 85 percent of female plants in the vicinity, but the female flowers "choose" which males will fertilize them.

• Marriage is a truce between genes. Human males benefit from a social structure that enables almost all of them to mate, not just the "alpha males". Without this, most would live alone or in all-male groups.

• Males produce billions of sperm. In many species they try to father as many genetic offspring as possible.

• Females produce fewer ova than the male does sperm, so try to ensure their eggs are successfully fertilized and that they become adults. Females seek impregnation by higher-ranking males; even amongst monogamous bird species, up to 40 percent of the young may be fathered by another male, because female birds routinely attempt to gain both a reliable mate and the best sperm available. In the UK, up to 20 percent of children are not the offspring of their ostensible fathers.

• Concealed ovulation is found in humans, the orang-utan, some monkeys and nearly all birds. If males do not know when their partners are fertile, they stay around more, and end up helping to look after the children. Concealed ovulation means that males cannot be certain of paternity, and enables females to keep secret their choice of mate.

• If a partner is unfaithful, females lose no genetic investment, but males risk bringing up alien offspring. Men try to guard their wives with veils, purdah, female circumcision, and chastity belts; they are violent towards their wives' lovers and copulate with their wives frequently, not just while they are fertile.

human asexual
reproduction (cloning)

humans appeared

primates appeared

sexual reproduction
in animals

life on land

marine animals

some plants
changed from
asexual to
sexual reproduction

life appeared

earth formed

SEXUAL REPRODUCTION

• Creation of new variants make extinction less likely through better adaptation to changing environments.

• Combination of genes from two sources accelerates the rate of evolution.

• Dilution of disadvantageous genes.

• Reduced damage to DNA.

• Reduced susceptibility to parasites.

but:

• Mates may be scarce or uncooperative.

• Reliance on other species to effect mating, such as pollination depending on bees.

• Genes that interact beneficially in the parent may be separated.

ADVANTAGES AND DISADVANTAGES OF SEXUAL AND ASEXUAL REPRODUCTION

Sexual and asexual reproduction are found in both the animal and plant kingdom. Most species of animals which exhibit asexual reproduction can also reproduce sexually.

ASEXUAL REPRODUCTION

• Allows for rapid increases in the number of individuals.

• Uses less energy, requires less time, does not require a mate, and all genetic material is passed to the next generation.

• More vulnerable to unfavorable environmental conditions, such as climate.

HUMANS
Testicular size directly relates to the amount of sperm competition from other males. In primates, the proportionately larger the testes, the more polygamous or promiscuous.

The human male hangs halfway between a pygmy chimp (largest) and gorilla or gibbon (smallest).

PRIMATES
Apes have a hard bone in the penis, unlike men.

Gorillas mate roughly 10 times per pregnancy, chimps 1,000 times, and bonobo (pygmy chimps) 5,000 times.

Bonobo and humans are the only two species that sometimes have sex face to face.

MAMMALS
Only 3 percent stay with one partner for life.

FISH
Female fish and some lizards only ovulate by the act of copulation or in the presence of male sperm.

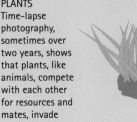

PLANTS
Time-lapse photography, sometimes over two years, shows that plants, like animals, compete with each other for resources and mates, invade new territory, and form partnerships.

13

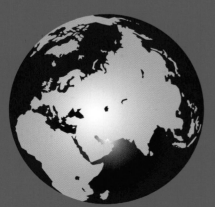

Part One SEXUALITY

"I regard sex like a glass of water, from
which I drink when I am thirsty."

— Alexandra Kollontai (1872–1952)
letter to Lenin

PUBERTY

Puberty starts in the brain. The hypothalamus stimulates the pituitary gland which in turn acts on the ovaries or testes to set puberty into motion. Puberty usually starts between the ages of 8 and 13 years in girls and between 9 and 14 in boys. Some adolescents complete the process before others even begin. By the age of 20 most have reached the end of puberty. In many industrialized countries puberty occurs about two years earlier than it did 100 years ago. This is generally attributed to better nutrition, environmental, and genetic factors.

Many infants have erections and fondle themselves. But unlike all other animals, and for reasons that are not clear, sexual development in humans then goes on hold for about 10 years.

All cultures embrace rituals linked to puberty. These rites of passage are more common for girls than for boys.

Puberty is
getting younger:

UK 1500
average age 19

UK 1890
average age 15

UK 1998
average age 13

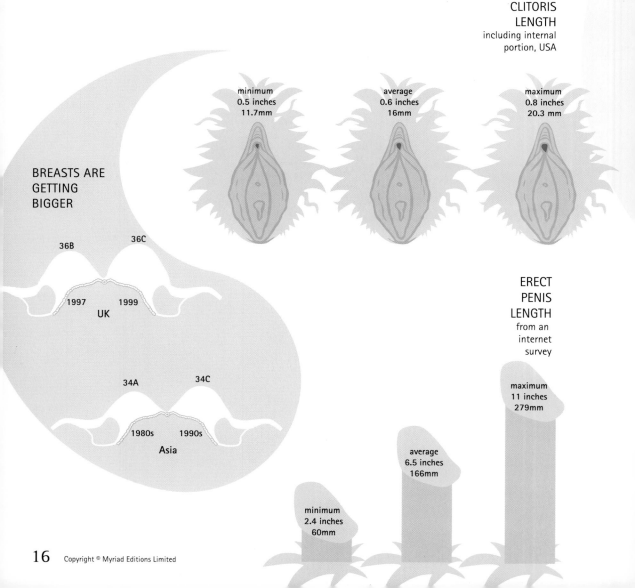

CLITORIS
LENGTH
including internal
portion, USA

minimum
0.5 inches
11.7mm

average
0.6 inches
16mm

maximum
0.8 inches
20.3 mm

BREASTS ARE
GETTING
BIGGER

36B

36C

1997   1999
UK

34A   34C

1980s   1990s
Asia

ERECT
PENIS
LENGTH
from an
internet
survey

maximum
11 inches
279mm

average
6.5 inches
166mm

minimum
2.4 inches
60mm

brain
8-13 years old
produces hormones
to initiate
puberty

brain
9-14 years old
produces hormones
to initiate
puberty

facial hair
13-15 years old
first appears

breasts
8-10 years old
the nipples bud

10-12 years old
breast bud; may be
asymmetrical at first

12-14 years old
breasts develop further;
nipples become darker

16-18 years old
breasts fully
mature

skin
13-15 years old
half of all girls
develop acne

skin
16-17 years old
most boys
develop acne

voice
13-15 years old
deepens with the
growth of the larynx

15 years old
average age at which
voice "breaks"

fat
8-10 years old
begins to be deposited

13-17 years old
increase in fat on hips
and breasts

armpit hair
12-14 years old
begins to grow

pelvic bones
8-10 years old
start to grow into
female shape

armpit hair
13-15 years old
begins to grow

breasts
12-14 years old
enlarges in up to
one-third of boys

14-17 years old
enlargement returns
to normal

uterus
7-9 years old
begins to grow

estrogen
7-9 years old
starts to increase

10-12 years old
marked increases

11-14 years old
now behaves
cyclically, even before
first period

menarche
10-16 years old
menstruation begins;
menstrual cycles may
occur without an egg
being released

12-15 years old
earliest normal
pregnancies

pubic hair
10-12 years old
first appears

11-14 years old
abundant and curly

genitalia
11-14 years old
grow and develop

vagina
11-14 years old
walls thicken and
secretions appear;
vagina changes from
alkaline to acid

pubic hair
11-14 years old
first appears

13-16 years old
abundant and
curly

testes
9-15 years old
start growing

12-15 years old
rapid growth

sperm
11-16 years old
production begins

12-17 years old
onset of nocturnal
emissions
(wet dreams)

11-17 years old
mature sperm
produced

penis
9-15 years old
blood supply
to the penis
and scrotum
increases

12-15 years old
rapid growth
of penis

prostate gland
11-14 years old
starts to
function

bones
16-18 years old
skeletal growth ends

bones
17-21 years old
skeletal growth ends

FIRST ENCOUNTERS

Sexual initiation is determined as much by culture as by gender.

In many countries there is little difference between the age at which men and women first experience sexual intercourse. The Middle East and Catholic countries, such as Brazil, Italy, Peru, and Portugal, practice stricter sexual codes for women and this is reflected in the later age of first sex.

More countries report the age of first sex for women than for men, because of the possibility of pregnancy. In Brazil, Japan, and the USA, there are more sexually-active men than women. The pattern is reversed in Ghana, partly because young women tend to marry earlier.

Teenagers have sex at an earlier age than their parents' generation, but this trend may be levelling off and even reversing in some countries.

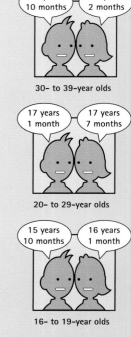

18 years 4 months / 18 years 11 months
40- to 45-year olds

17 years 10 months / 18 years 2 months
30- to 39-year olds

17 years 1 month / 17 years 7 months
20- to 29-year olds

15 years 10 months / 16 years 1 month
16- to 19-year olds

STARTING YOUNGER
Average age of first sexual intercourse by generation
15 countries

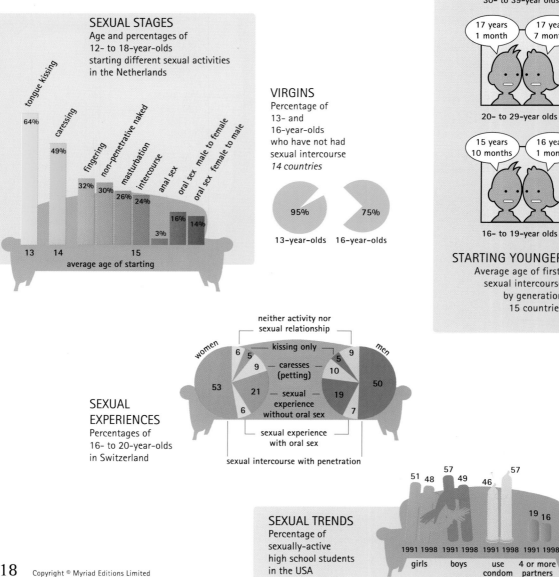

SEXUAL STAGES
Age and percentages of 12- to 18-year-olds starting different sexual activities in the Netherlands

tongue kissing 64%
caressing 49%
fingering 32%
non-penetrative naked 30%
masturbation 26%
intercourse 24%
anal sex 3%
oral sex male to female 16%
oral sex female to male 14%

13   14   15
average age of starting

VIRGINS
Percentage of 13- and 16-year-olds who have not had sexual intercourse
14 countries

95% 13-year-olds   75% 16-year-olds

SEXUAL EXPERIENCES
Percentages of 16- to 20-year-olds in Switzerland

women — men

neither activity nor sexual relationship
kissing only
caresses (petting)
sexual experience without oral sex
sexual experience with oral sex
sexual intercourse with penetration

women: 6 5 9 53 21 6
men: 9 5 10 50 19 7

SEXUAL TRENDS
Percentage of sexually-active high school students in the USA

51 48   57 49   46   57   19 16
1991 1998 1991 1998 1991 1998 1991 1998
girls   boys   use   4 or more
                       condom   partners

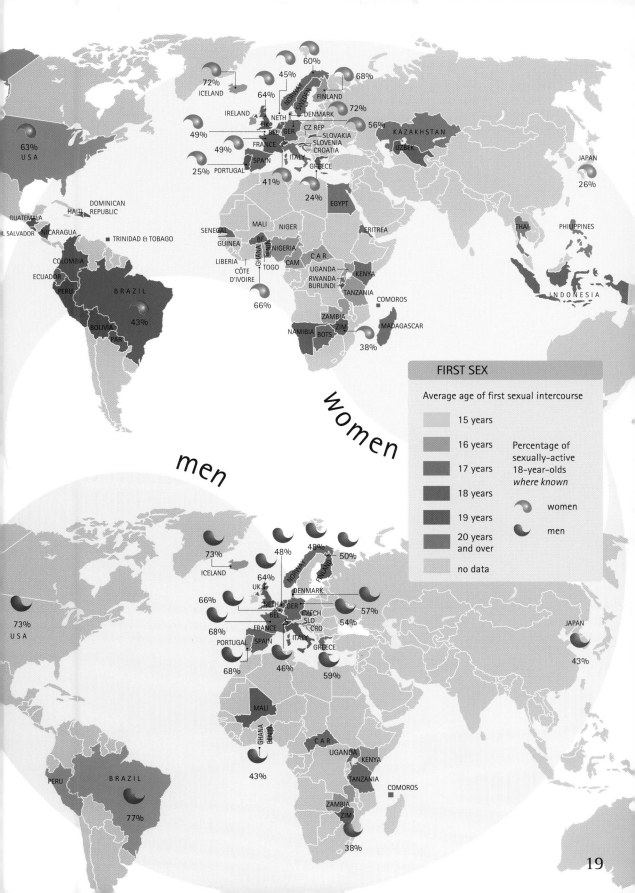

FIRST SEX

Average age of first sexual intercourse

- 15 years
- 16 years
- 17 years
- 18 years
- 19 years
- 20 years and over
- no data

Percentage of sexually-active 18-year-olds *where known*

- women
- men

women

men

72% ICELAND
60%
45%
68%
64% NORWAY SWEDEN FINLAND
72% DENMARK
IRELAND
49% UK NETH GER
BEL CZ REP
49% FRANCE SLOVAKIA
SLOVENIA
CROATIA
25% PORTUGAL
SPAIN ITALY
41% GREECE
24% EGYPT
56% KAZAKHSTAN
UZBEK
63% USA
JAPAN
26%

DOMINICAN REPUBLIC
GUATEMALA HAITI
SALVADOR NICARAGUA
TRINIDAD & TOBAGO
COLOMBIA
ECUADOR
PERU BRAZIL
43%
BOLIVIA
PAR

SENEGAL MALI NIGER ERITREA
GUINEA BF NIGERIA
LIBERIA GHANA BENIN
CÔTE TOGO CAM C A R
D'IVOIRE
66%
UGANDA KENYA
RWANDA
BURUNDI TANZANIA
COMOROS
ZAMBIA MADAGASCAR
NAMIBIA ZIM
BOTS
38%

THAI PHILIPPINES
INDONESIA

73% ICELAND
48% 48%
50%
64% NORWAY FINLAND
UK DENMARK
66% NETH GER
BEL 57%
68% FRANCE CZECH SLO
SPAIN ITALY CRO 54%
PORTUGAL
68% 46% GREECE
59%
JAPAN
43%

73% USA

PERU BRAZIL
77%

MALI
GHANA BENIN
C A R
UGANDA KENYA
43% TANZANIA
COMOROS
ZAMBIA
ZIM
38%

19

SEXUAL PRACTICES

Every day, 120 million acts of sexual intercourse take place around the world. During their lifetime, the average person in the UK will have sex 2,580 times with five different people.

USA 1996:
46% of women agree that "a good night's sleep is better than sex".

28 USA

MEXICO

17

23 CANADA

USA 1990s:
15% of adults are having half of all the sex.

France 1997:
20% said they had no interest in sex.

15 SPAIN

21 UNITED KINGDOM

16 FRANCE

17 GERMANY

14 ITALY

15 POLAND

12 RUSSIA

13 Hong Kong

India 1996:
76% of newly weds in Calcutta do not have sex on their wedding night.

10 THAILAND

INDIA

NUMBER OF SEX PARTNERS

Reported by 34,500 internet users, half of whom are under 25 years old

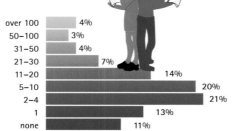

over 100	4%
50–100	3%
31–50	4%
21–30	7%
11–20	14%
5–10	20%
2–4	21%
1	13%
none	11%

BONDAGE

Preference of dominant or submissive roles, by gender and sexual orientation, of international discussion group on sexual bondage

■ prefer dominant

□ prefer submissive

88% / 12%
male homosexuals

71% / 29%
male heterosexuals

89% / 11%
female heterosexuals

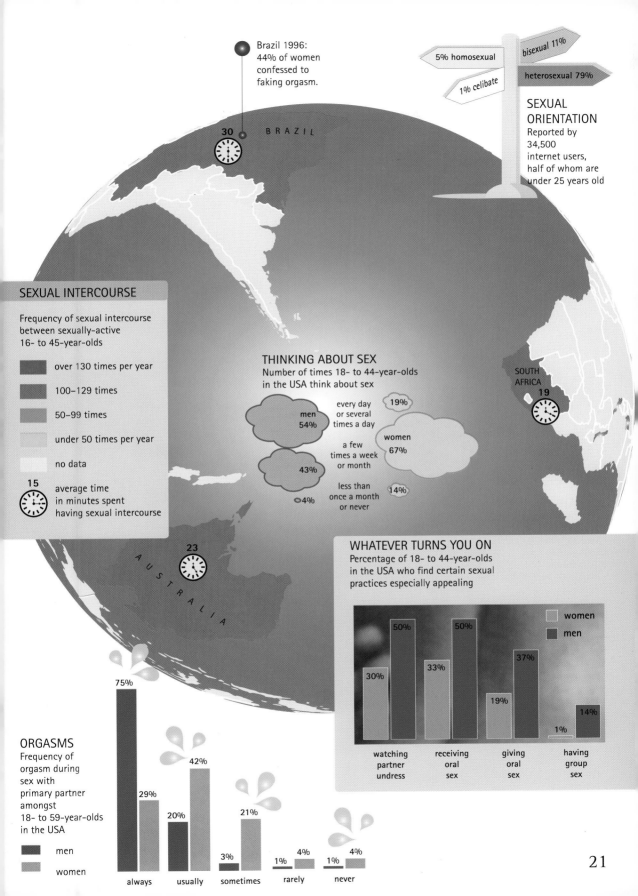

Brazil 1996:
44% of women
confessed to
faking orgasm.

30
BRAZIL

5% homosexual
bisexual 11%
1% celibate
heterosexual 79%

SEXUAL ORIENTATION
Reported by
34,500
internet users,
half of whom are
under 25 years old

SEXUAL INTERCOURSE

Frequency of sexual intercourse
between sexually-active
16- to 45-year-olds

over 130 times per year

100–129 times

50–99 times

under 50 times per year

no data

15 average time
    in minutes spent
    having sexual intercourse

THINKING ABOUT SEX
Number of times 18- to 44-year-olds
in the USA think about sex

SOUTH
AFRICA
19

men
54%

women
67%

every day
or several
times a day   19%

a few
times a week
or month

43%

less than
once a month
or never   14%

4%

AUSTRALIA
23

WHATEVER TURNS YOU ON
Percentage of 18- to 44-year-olds
in the USA who find certain sexual
practices especially appealing

women
men

30%   50%   50%
              33%
       19%   37%
                     1%   14%

watching   receiving   giving   having
partner   oral   oral   group
undress   sex   sex   sex

ORGASMS
Frequency of
orgasm during
sex with
primary partner
amongst
18- to 59-year-olds
in the USA

men

women

75%
29%
20%   42%
3%   21%
1% 4%   1% 4%

always usually sometimes rarely never

21

HOMOSEXUALITY

Sex between consenting adults of the same sex in private is subject to legislation, violence, harassment – even the death penalty. Slowly this is changing.

GREENLAND
FAROE IS.
ICELAND
NORWAY
SWEDEN
FINLAND
ESTONIA
LATVIA
LITHUANIA
DENMARK
IRELAND
UNITED KINGDOM
GERMANY
NETHERLANDS
LUXEMBOURG
HUNGARY
FRANCE
SWITZ.
AUSTRIA
SLOVENIA
CROATIA
ROMAN
SLOVENIA
YUGOSLAVIA
BULGAR
ITALY
MONACO
ALBANIA
PORTUGAL
SPAIN
LIECHTENSTEIN

In 1791 France repealed a total ban on homosexuality.

CANADA

UNITED STATES OF AMERICA

BERMUDA

CUBA
BAHAMAS
TURKS AND CAICOS
CAYMAN IS.
JAMAICA
BR VIRGIN IS.
ANGUILLA
PUERTO RICO
ST KITTS AND NEVIS
MONTSERRAT
ST LUCIA
BARBADOS
ARUBA
GRENADA
NICARAGUA
TRINIDAD & TOBAGO
VENEZUELA
GUYANA
COLOMBIA
SURINAME
FRENCH GUIANA (Fr)
ECUADOR

BRAZIL

CHILE

ARGENTINA

MOROCCO
TUNISIA
ALGERIA
LIBYA
CAPE VERDE
MAURITANIA
MALI
CHAD
SENEGAL
GAMBIA
GUINEA-BISSAU
GUINEA
BURKINA FASO
SIERRA LEONE
LIBERIA
TOGO
BENIN
NIGERIA
CAMEROON
GABON
CONGO
ANGOLA
NAMIBIA
SOUTH AFRICA

Same-sex activity has been observed in 450 species of birds and mammals.

- Homosexual black swans are more successful at raising young than heterosexual pairs.
- Male orang-utans indulge in fellatio.
- Male walruses sodomize each other.
- In summer months, killer whales devote a tenth of their time to homosexual activity.

Between 3% and 4% of the world's male population, and between 1.5% and 2% of the world's female population, are living exclusively as homosexuals.

GAY PRIDE WORLDWIDE Countries where celebrations were held in 1999:
Argentina Australia Austria Belgium Brazil Canada Chile Colombia Denmark Ecuador France Germany Hong Kong Netherlands Norway New Zealand Paraguay Peru Philippines Poland Portugal Puerto Rico South Africa Spain Sweden

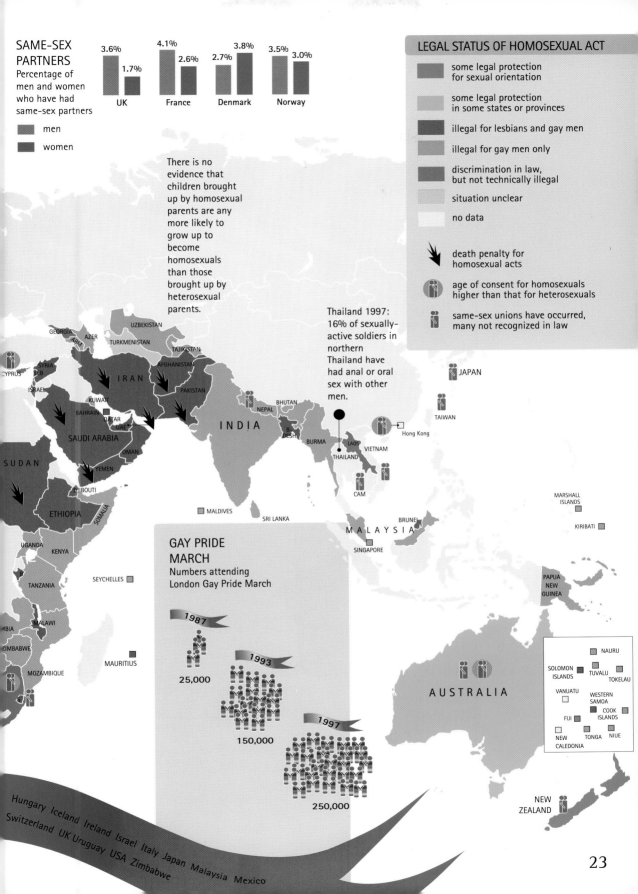

SAME-SEX PARTNERS

Percentage of men and women who have had same-sex partners

- men
- women

UK 3.6% / 1.7%
France 4.1% / 2.6%
Denmark 2.7% / 3.8%
Norway 3.5% / 3.0%

LEGAL STATUS OF HOMOSEXUAL ACT

- some legal protection for sexual orientation
- some legal protection in some states or provinces
- illegal for lesbians and gay men
- illegal for gay men only
- discrimination in law, but not technically illegal
- situation unclear
- no data

- death penalty for homosexual acts
- age of consent for homosexuals higher than that for heterosexuals
- same-sex unions have occurred, many not recognized in law

There is no evidence that children brought up by homosexual parents are any more likely to grow up to become homosexuals than those brought up by heterosexual parents.

Thailand 1997: 16% of sexually-active soldiers in northern Thailand have had anal or oral sex with other men.

GAY PRIDE MARCH

Numbers attending London Gay Pride March

1987 — 25,000
1993 — 150,000
1997 — 250,000

Hungary Iceland Ireland Israel Italy Japan Malaysia Mexico
Switzerland UK Uruguay USA Zimbabwe

CYPRUS, GEORGIA, AZER, ARM, SYRIA, LEB, ISRAEL, TURKMENISTAN, UZBEKISTAN, TAJIKISTAN, AFGHANISTAN, IRAN, KUWAIT, BAHRAIN, QATAR, UAE, SAUDI ARABIA, OMAN, YEMEN, PAKISTAN, INDIA, NEPAL, BHUTAN, BANGLADESH, BURMA, LAOS, VIETNAM, THAILAND, CAM, MALAYSIA, SINGAPORE, BRUNEI, SRI LANKA, MALDIVES, SUDAN, ETHIOPIA, SOMALIA, DJIBOUTI, UGANDA, KENYA, TANZANIA, MALAWI, ZIMBABWE, MOZAMBIQUE, SEYCHELLES, MAURITIUS, JAPAN, TAIWAN, Hong Kong, MARSHALL ISLANDS, KIRIBATI, PAPUA NEW GUINEA, AUSTRALIA, NEW ZEALAND

NAURU, SOLOMON ISLANDS, TUVALU, TOKELAU, VANUATU, WESTERN SAMOA, FIJI, COOK ISLANDS, NEW CALEDONIA, TONGA, NIUE

GREENLAND

ICELAND

CANADA

NORWAY
SWEDEN
FINLA

DENMARK
LA

IRELAND

UNITED STATES
OF AMERICA

UK
NETH
BEL GERMANY POLAND
CZ REP
FRANCE AUS HUN
LIECHTENSTEIN

PORTUGAL SPAIN ANDORRA
SAN MARINO ALB
ITALY
GREE

MALTA

Native
Americans

MEXICO

Estimated
numbers
worldwide:

- genetic,
  physical and
  hormonal
  gender
  complexities
  1 in every 60

- male to female
  transsexuals
  **1 in every
  12,000**

- female to male
  transsexuals
  **1 in every
  30,000**

GHANA

BRAZIL

A NEW IDENTITY

Documents reissued in the reassigned
sex of the transsexual person in Europe

The human population
is not divided simply into
males and females.
A person's sexual profile has
several components: their
physical makeup (chromosomal
sex, sex organs, genitalia), their
gender identity (self-image),
their social gender role (how they
behave), their sexual orientation
(which sex they find attractive).
These four components exist
independently. A person may
express any variation of each
of these in any combination.

all personal documents
may be reissued
following gender reassignment

some personal documents
may be reissued

legal situation unclear on
gender reassignment and/or
document reissue

gender reassignment illegal

no data

SOUT
AFRIC

ARGENTINA

 illegal to change birth certificate or
marry following gender reassignment

legal
or openly performed
without prosecution

legal in some states
or provinces

illegal

no data
or legal situation unclear

societies in which
transgender people
have an accepted place

RUSSIA

UKRAINE
MOL

TURKEY

CYPRUS
ISRAEL

IRAQ

IRAN

EGYPT

KUWAIT

BAHRAIN

QATAR
UAE

SAUDI ARABIA

OMAN

INDIA

BURMA

CHINA

JAPAN

TAIWAN

HONG KONG
SAR

PHILIPPINES

THAILAND

SRI LANKA

BRUNEI

MALAYSIA

SINGAPORE

INDONESIA

WESTERN
SAMOA

POLYNESIA

KENYA

MAURITIUS

MADAGASCAR

ICELAND

IRELAND

UK

NORWAY

SWEDEN

FINLAND

EST

LAT

LITH

DENMARK

BELARUS

RUSSIA

NETH

BEL

GERMANY

POLAND

CZ

SL

UKRAINE

MOL

AUSTRALIA

FRANCE

LIECHTENSTEIN

SWITZ

AUST

HUNG

ROM

GEO

NEW
ZEALAND

MONACO

ANDORRA

SAN MARINO

S C

B-H

YUG

BULGARIA

PORTUGAL

SPAIN

ITALY

ALB

M

GREECE

TURKEY

MALTA

CYPRUS

25

Part Two MATING

"There is no greater nor keener pleasure than that of bodily love –
and none which is more irrational."

– Plato, The Republic III,
Greece, 427-347 BC

SEX APPEAL

Sex appeal remains largely undefinable, although men and women themselves know when it is there. The sexual spark between two people depends as much on personality as on physical appearance. Sex appeal is subjective: a man or woman may have sex appeal for one person but hold no appeal for another.

Some elements of sex appeal have been identified and researched. Only symmetry and waist-to-hip ratio have been measured across cultures: the findings are surprisingly universal, such as a preferred 70 percent waist-to-hip ratio, irrespective of culture or weight. Animals as well as humans show a marked preference for others with symmetrical features.

Physical attractiveness is a significant component of sex appeal. Worldwide, physically attractive men tend to be slightly above average height and have prominent cheekbones, a large jaw, and a fairly muscular torso. In women, large eyes, a small nose, full lips, firm symmetrical breasts, and unblemished skin are favored. Such concepts of attractiveness vary between cultures and even over time within the same culture.

While models and idealized images of beauty are getting thinner, most women are getting fatter. Liposuction, the surgical removal of fat, is the most common plastic surgery procedure in the USA. Increasingly, men as well as women are opting to reconstruct their appeal: nine percent of all cosmetic procedures are performed on men.

Body odors are another important aspect of sex appeal. Androstenol and androstenone are steroids present in human armpit perspiration, and these "pheromes" are substances that may influence sexual behavior. Pheromes have been found to control the sex life of some animals; their influence on human sexual behavior is still unclear.

Sex appeal, or sexual chemistry, may be more than skin deep. Research shows that different neurochemical transmitters in the human brain flicker during infatuation, enduring love, and plain lust.

UK:
22% of women consider shoulder blades the most attractive part of the male physique.

UK:
32% of men prefer women with large breasts.

USA:
Good-looking people earn 12% more than others.

Japan:
40% of men pluck their eyebrows.

Japan:
1% of young women are anorexic.

In 11 countries across Africa, the Americas, Asia, Australasia, and Europe, men prefer women's waist measurement to be 70% that of their hips.

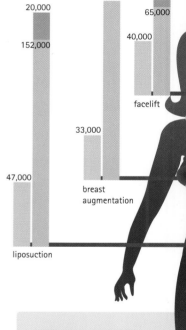

132,000
6,000
20,000
65,000
40,000
152,000

facelift

33,000

47,000

breast augmentation

liposuction

COSMETIC SURGERY
in the USA

Increasing numbers of men and women undergoing plastic and reconstructive surgery: 1998 compared with 1992

1992 men and women

1998 women

1998 men

THE SUCCESS OF SYMMETRY

The greater the man's symmetry:
- the earlier he loses his virginity
- the more quickly he gets women into bed
- the more sexual partners he has
- the more orgasms he occasions in women partners
- the more likely he is to be unfaithful

Symmetry in a woman's features is:
- related to her physical attractiveness but
- not correlated to the number of her sexual partners
- not correlated to her fidelity

Symmetry in animals is related to seductiveness, as found in 65 studies of 42 species.

16,000

104,000

60,000

3,000

63,000

eyelid surgery

19,000

chemical peel

chemical peel full face **$1,400**
collagen injection (per 1cc) **$300**
dermabrasion **$1,600**
eyelid surgery **$3,000**
nose reshaping **$3,400**
facelift **$5,000**
laser skin resurfacing face **$2,800**
male-pattern baldness **$2,800 – $4,200**
wrinkle injection **$400**

breast augmentation **$3,100**
breast reduction **$5,500**
liposuction **$1,900**
tummy tuck **$4,100**
buttock lift **$3,700**

THE COST OF SURGERY
in the USA

The average cost of plastic and reconstructive surgery

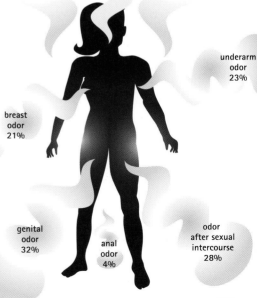

body odor with perfume
46%

body odor without perfume
48%

breath
16%

underarm odor
23%

breast odor
21%

SEXUAL SMELL

Percentage of men and women in Germany who find body odors sexually stimulating

genital odor
32%

anal odor
4%

odor after sexual intercourse
28%

29

DATING

In many countries and cultures dating is the accepted method of meeting a potential partner, with dates arranged in a variety of ways, including via email and the internet. As 60 percent of marriages worldwide are arranged, however, it is the minority of people who go on dates.

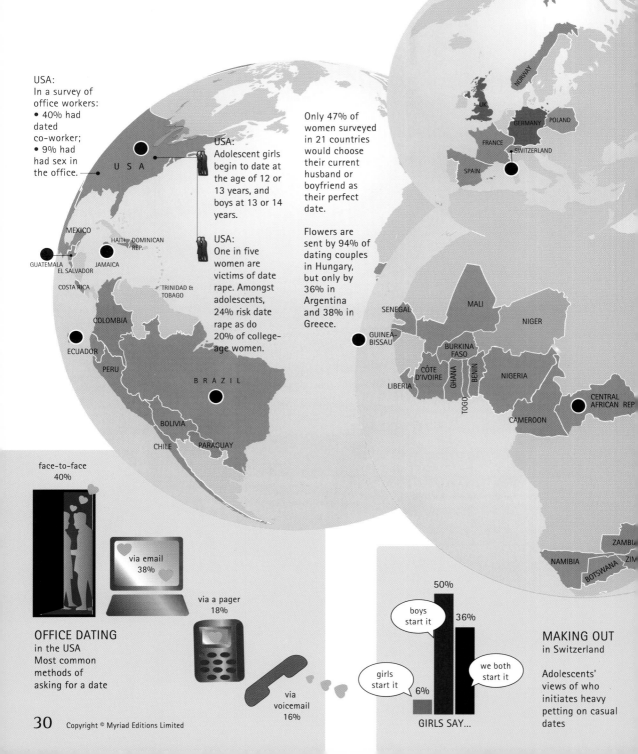

USA:
In a survey of office workers:
• 40% had dated co-worker;
• 9% had had sex in the office.

USA:
Adolescent girls begin to date at the age of 12 or 13 years, and boys at 13 or 14 years.

USA:
One in five women are victims of date rape. Amongst adolescents, 24% risk date rape as do 20% of college-age women.

Only 47% of women surveyed in 21 countries would choose their current husband or boyfriend as their perfect date.

Flowers are sent by 94% of dating couples in Hungary, but only by 36% in Argentina and 38% in Greece.

USA
MEXICO
GUATEMALA
EL SALVADOR
COSTA RICA
HAITI
DOMINICAN REP.
JAMAICA
TRINIDAD & TOBAGO
COLOMBIA
ECUADOR
PERU
BRAZIL
BOLIVIA
CHILE
PARAGUAY

NORWAY
UK
GERMANY
POLAND
FRANCE
SWITZERLAND
SPAIN

SENEGAL
GUINEA-BISSAU
MALI
NIGER
BURKINA FASO
CÔTE D'IVOIRE
GHANA
BENIN
NIGERIA
LIBERIA
TOGO
CAMEROON
CENTRAL AFRICAN REP
ZAMBIA
NAMIBIA
BOTSWANA
ZIM

OFFICE DATING
in the USA
Most common methods of asking for a date

face-to-face
40%

via email
38%

via a pager
18%

via voicemail
16%

MAKING OUT
in Switzerland

Adolescents' views of who initiates heavy petting on casual dates

boys start it
50%

we both start it
36%

girls start it
6%

GIRLS SAY...

INTERNET DATING

Internet survey of 34,500 respondents between 1995 and 1999.

- 12% — had sex with someone met online
- 11% — responded to an online personal ad
- 10% — placed an online personal ad

SEX ON A DATE

Percentage of women under 20 who have sex outside marriage

- over 70%
- 50%–69%
- 30%–49%
- 10%–29%
- under 10%

● over 50% of men under 20 have sex outside marriage *where known*

WHERE PARTNERS FIRST MEET
in the USA

	married	cohabiting	non-cohabiting partnerships lasting more than one month	non-cohabiting partnerships lasting less than one month
school	23%	10%	22%	22%
work	15%	18%	17%	11%
private social venue	14%	19%	20%	29%
public social venue	10%	14%	16%	20%
church	8%	2%	2%	1%
elsewhere	30%	37%	23%	17%

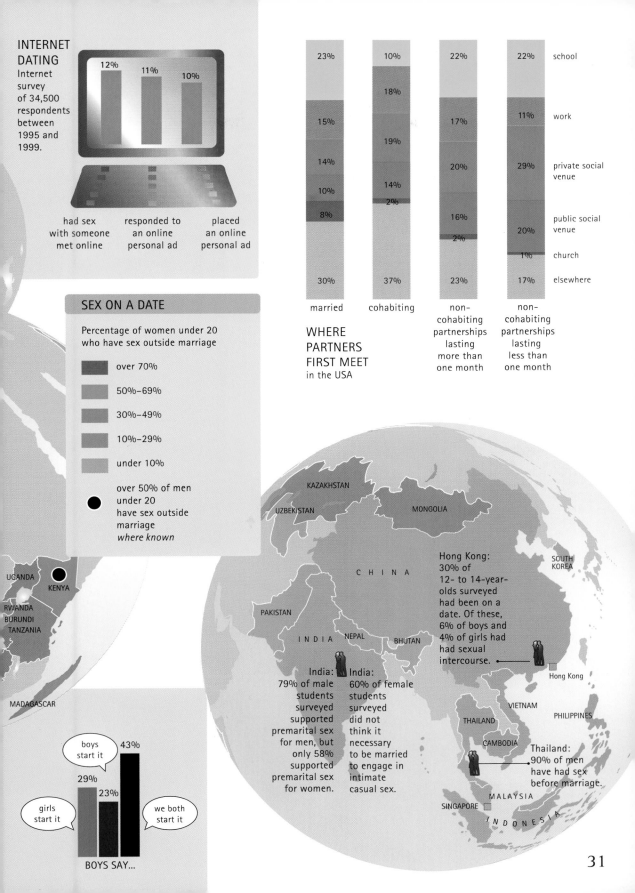

KAZAKHSTAN

UZBEKISTAN

MONGOLIA

CHINA

PAKISTAN

INDIA NEPAL BHUTAN

SOUTH KOREA

Hong Kong: 30% of 12- to 14-year-olds surveyed had been on a date. Of these, 6% of boys and 4% of girls had had sexual intercourse.

Hong Kong

India: 79% of male students surveyed supported premarital sex for men, but only 58% supported premarital sex for women.

India: 60% of female students surveyed did not think it necessary to be married to engage in intimate casual sex.

VIETNAM

THAILAND

CAMBODIA

PHILIPPINES

Thailand: 90% of men have had sex before marriage.

MALAYSIA

SINGAPORE

INDONESIA

UGANDA
KENYA
RWANDA
BURUNDI
TANZANIA
MADAGASCAR

BOYS SAY...

- boys start it — 29%
- girls start it — 23%
- we both start it — 43%

31

CHOOSE YOUR PARTNER

Worldwide, men prefer younger women and women prefer older men. Men prize physical attraction, while women look for providers.

Worldwide: 60% of marriages are still arranged.

Gambia 1993: One in three women were neither asked for their consent nor knew they were married until the ceremony was over.

QUALITIES SOUGHT IN A MATE
Preference ratings in 33 countries

men and women look for:
1 mutual attraction
2 dependable character
3 emotional stability and maturity
4 pleasing disposition

men look for:		women look for:
good health	5	education and intelligence
education and intelligence	6	sociability
sociability	7	good health
desire for home and children	8	desire for home and children
refinement, neatness	9	ambition and industriousness
good looks	10	refinement, neatness
ambition and industriousness	11	similar education
good cook and housekeeper	12	good financial prospects
good financial prospects	13	good looks
similar education	14	favorable social status or rating
favorable social status or rating	15	good cook and housekeeper
chastity	16	similar religious background
similar religious background	17	similar political background
similar political background	18	chastity

NOT JUST A PRETTY FACE
Lowest acceptable intelligence, on a scale out of 100, for various mating rituals

high intelligence

	women's intelligence acceptable to men	men's intelligence acceptable to women	
marriage	67	66	marriage
steady dating	63	62	steady dating
		55	sexual intercourse
dating	51	49	dating
sexual intercourse	44		

low intelligence

TRAFFIC IN MAIL-ORDER BRIDES

South Korea 1999:
The 14th-century law forbidding marriage between couples with the same surname was finally revoked.

China 1990s:
80% of marriages were arranged, 60% by a matchmaker, 20% by the couple's parents.

CHINA

SOUTH KOREA

JAPAN

IRAN

ISRAEL

INDIA

TAIWAN

INDONESIA

AUSTRALIA

NEW ZEALAND

AIR MAIL
USA *1990s*
brides from South East Asia, China, Korea and Colombia

AIR MAIL
Germany *1990*
1,267 brides from Philippines

AIR MAIL
Italy *1991*
5,000 brides from Nigeria

AIR MAIL
Finland *1990s*
brides from Philippines, Thailand and eastern Europe

AIR MAIL
South Africa *1992*
brides from Mozambique

AIR MAIL
Australia, Norway *1990s*
"contact clubs" arrange Philippine sex tours to meet potential brides

OLDER MEN, YOUNGER WOMEN

Men look for spouses:

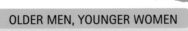

more than 6 years younger than themselves

4 to 6 years younger

2 to 4 years younger

less than 2 years younger

no data

good looks in a partner are significantly more important for men than for women

good financial prospects in a partner are significantly more important for women than for men

33

MARRIAGE

The average age of marriage varies from under 16 to almost 30 years old. In many countries, the youngest couples are married without the consent of the girl concerned. Worldwide, 60 percent of marriages are arranged.

Canada:
Without parental consent, the legal age of marriage is 18 years old.

USA:
With parental consent, marriage can take place in some states as young as 12 (girls) and 14 (boys).

CANADA

USA

MEXICO

GUATEMALA
EL SALVADOR
NICARAGUA
COSTA RICA
PANAMA

HONDURAS

CUBA
JAMAICA
HAITI

DOMINICAN
REPUBLIC

VENEZUELA

BARBADOS
TRINIDAD & TOBAGO
GUYANA

COLOMBIA

ECUADOR

Surui

PERU

BRAZIL

BOLIVIA

PARAGUAY

CHILE

ARGENTINA

URUGUAY

ICELAND

NORWAY
SWEDEN

DENMARK
IRELAND
UK
NETH
BEL
GERMANY
FRANCE
POL
CZ REP
AUS
ITALY
SPAIN
PORTUGAL
ALBANIA

CANARY IS.

WESTERN
SAHARA

MOROCCO

TUNISIA

ALGERIA

LIBYA

MAURITANIA

SENEGAL
GAMBIA
GUINEA-
BISSAU
GUINEA
SIERRA
LEONE
LIBERIA

MALI

BURKINA
FASO

CÔTE
D'IVOIRE

GHANA
TOGO
BENIN

NIGERIA

CAMEROON
EQUATORIAL
GUINEA
GABON

CONGO

NAMIBIA

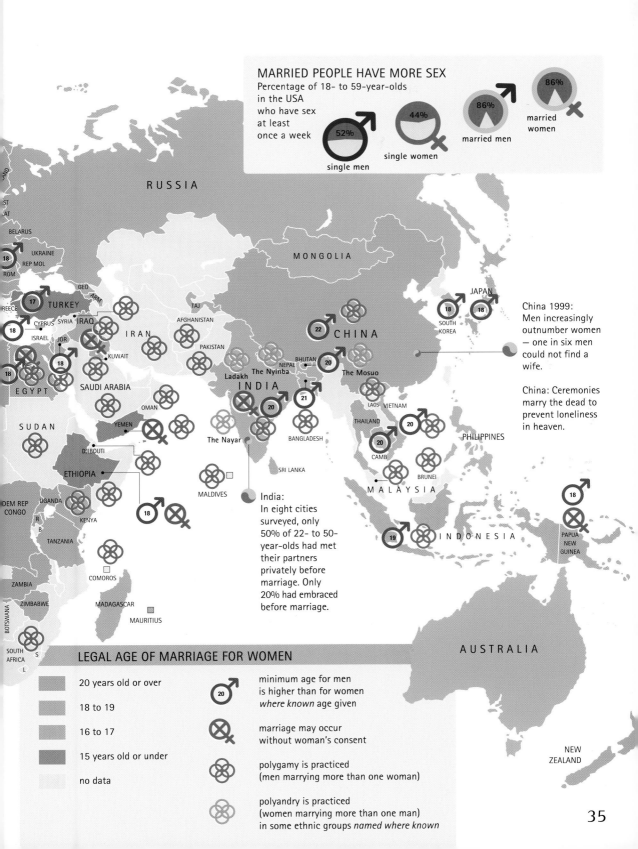

MARRIED PEOPLE HAVE MORE SEX

Percentage of 18- to 59-year-olds in the USA who have sex at least once a week

52% single men

44% single women

86% married men

86% married women

China 1999: Men increasingly outnumber women — one in six men could not find a wife.

China: Ceremonies marry the dead to prevent loneliness in heaven.

India: In eight cities surveyed, only 50% of 22- to 50-year-olds had met their partners privately before marriage. Only 20% had embraced before marriage.

LEGAL AGE OF MARRIAGE FOR WOMEN

- 20 years old or over
- 18 to 19
- 16 to 17
- 15 years old or under
- no data

minimum age for men is higher than for women *where known* age given

marriage may occur without woman's consent

polygamy is practiced (men marrying more than one woman)

polyandry is practiced (women marrying more than one man) in some ethnic groups *named where known*

35

ADULTERY

Adultery is universal. In general, men committing adultery are treated more leniently than women.

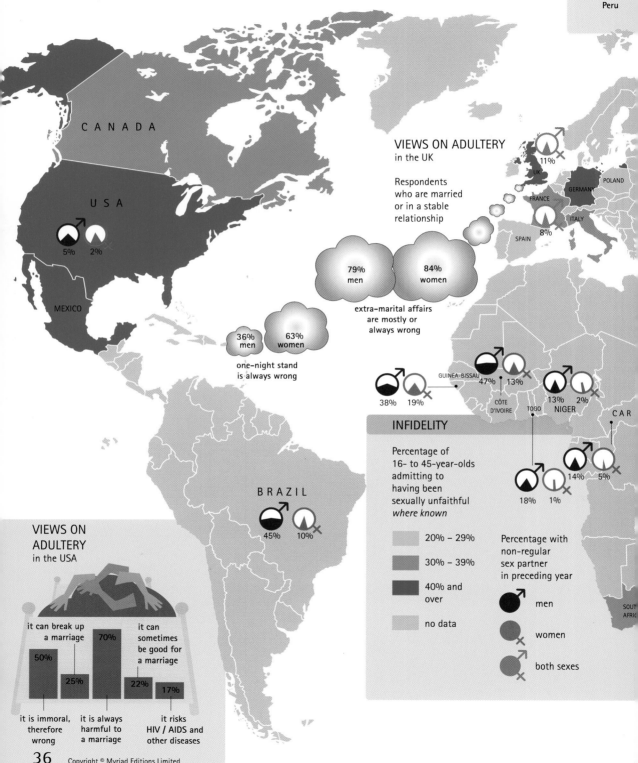

67%

Peru

VIEWS ON ADULTERY
in the UK

Respondents who are married or in a stable relationship

11% UK

POLAND

GERMANY

8% FRANCE

ITALY

SPAIN

79% men

84% women

extra-marital affairs are mostly or always wrong

CANADA

USA

5%   **2%**

MEXICO

36% men   **63% women**

one-night stand is always wrong

GUINEA-BISSAU

38%   **19%**

47%   **13%**
CÔTE D'IVOIRE

TOGO

13%   **2%**
NIGER

C A R

18%   **1%**

14%   **5%**

BRAZIL

45%   **10%**

INFIDELITY

Percentage of 16- to 45-year-olds admitting to having been sexually unfaithful *where known*

- 20% – 29%
- 30% – 39%
- 40% and over
- no data

Percentage with non-regular sex partner in preceding year

- men
- women
- both sexes

SOUTH AFRICA

VIEWS ON ADULTERY
in the USA

it can break up a marriage

50%

it is immoral, therefore wrong

25%

it is always harmful to a marriage

70%

it can sometimes be good for a marriage

22%

it risks HIV / AIDS and other diseases

17%

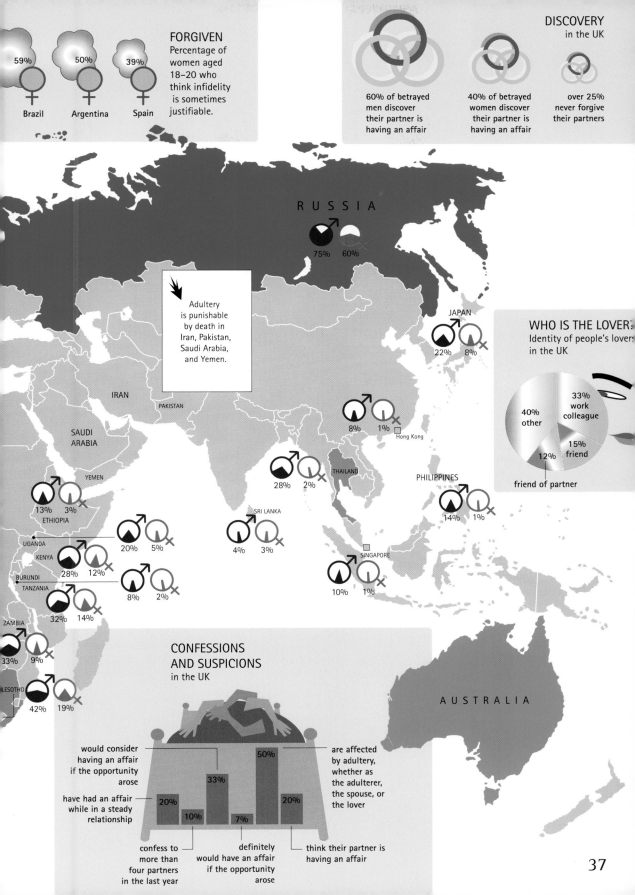

FORGIVEN
Percentage of women aged 18–20 who think infidelity is sometimes justifiable.

59% Brazil
50% Argentina
39% Spain

DISCOVERY
in the UK

60% of betrayed men discover their partner is having an affair

40% of betrayed women discover their partner is having an affair

over 25% never forgive their partners

RUSSIA
75%   60%

Adultery is punishable by death in Iran, Pakistan, Saudi Arabia, and Yemen.

JAPAN
22%   8%

IRAN

PAKISTAN

SAUDI ARABIA

YEMEN

8%   1%
Hong Kong

THAILAND

28%   2%

PHILIPPINES

13%   3%
ETHIOPIA

20%   5%

UGANDA

KENYA

28%   12%

SRI LANKA
4%   3%

14%   1%

BURUNDI

TANZANIA

8%   2%

SINGAPORE

10%   1%

32%   14%

ZAMBIA

33%   9%

LESOTHO

42%   19%

WHO IS THE LOVER?
Identity of people's lovers in the UK

40% other
33% work colleague
15% friend
12% friend of partner

AUSTRALIA

CONFESSIONS AND SUSPICIONS
in the UK

would consider having an affair if the opportunity arose — 33%

have had an affair while in a steady relationship — 20%

confess to more than four partners in the last year — 10%

definitely would have an affair if the opportunity arose — 7%

50% — are affected by adultery, whether as the adulterer, the spouse, or the lover

20% — think their partner is having an affair

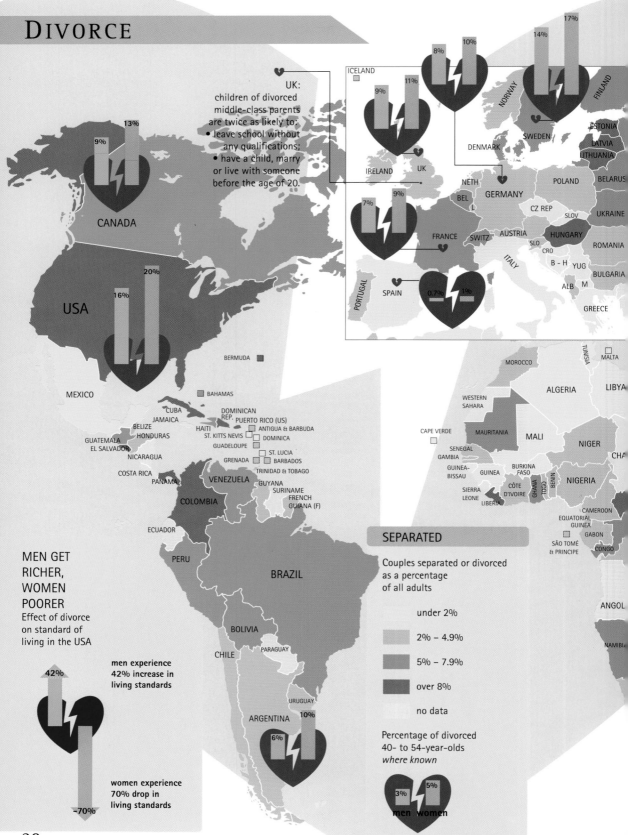

UK:
children of divorced
middle-class parents
are twice as likely to:
• leave school without
any qualifications;
• have a child, marry
or live with someone
before the age of 20.

ICELAND

9% 11%

8% 10%

14% 17%

NORWAY

FINLAND

SWEDEN

ESTONIA

DENMARK

LATVIA

LITHUANIA

IRELAND UK

NETH

GERMANY POLAND BELARUS

BEL

CZ REP

UKRAINE

7% 9%

SLOV

FRANCE

SWITZ AUSTRIA HUNGARY

ROMANIA

SLO

ITALY

CRO

B-H YUG

BULGARIA

PORTUGAL

SPAIN

0.7% 1%

ALB M

GREECE

CANADA

13%

9%

USA

16% 20%

MEXICO

BERMUDA

BAHAMAS

CUBA

DOMINICAN
REP.

JAMAICA

PUERTO RICO (US)

BELIZE

HAITI

ANTIGUA & BARBUDA

HONDURAS

ST. KITTS NEVIS

DOMINICA

GUATEMALA

GUADELOUPE

EL SALVADOR

ST. LUCIA

NICARAGUA

GRENADA

BARBADOS

COSTA RICA

TRINIDAD & TOBAGO

PANAMA

VENEZUELA

GUYANA

COLOMBIA

SURINAME

FRENCH
GUIANA (F)

ECUADOR

PERU

BRAZIL

BOLIVIA

CHILE

PARAGUAY

URUGUAY

ARGENTINA

10%

6%

TUNISIA

MALTA

MOROCCO

ALGERIA

LIBYA

WESTERN
SAHARA

CAPE VERDE

MAURITANIA

MALI

NIGER

CHA

SENEGAL

GAMBIA

GUINEA-
BISSAU

GUINEA

BURKINA
FASO

NIGERIA

SIERRA
LEONE

CÔTE
D'IVOIRE

GHANA

TOGO

BENIN

LIBERIA

CAMEROON

EQUATORIAL
GUINEA

GABON

SÃO TOMÉ
& PRINCIPE

CONGO

ANGOL

NAMIBIA

MEN GET RICHER, WOMEN POORER

Effect of divorce
on standard of
living in the USA

42%

men experience
42% increase in
living standards

−70%

women experience
70% drop in
living standards

SEPARATED

Couples separated or divorced
as a percentage
of all adults

under 2%

2% – 4.9%

5% – 7.9%

over 8%

no data

Percentage of divorced
40- to 54-year-olds
where known

3% 5%

men women

Divorce is almost unknown in some parts of the world, but increasingly common in others. Sexual problems and infidelity frequently are cited as grounds for divorce; whether these are the cause or effect of marriage breakdown is less clear.

RUSSIA

9%
13%

JAPAN

3%
5%

CHINA

1.4%
0.4%

China 1997:
The number of divorces totalled 1.9 million, more than twice as many as in 1985.

INDIA

1%
0.4%

MALDIVES

Malaysia:
60% of divorced women in Selangor turn to prostitution because of economic hardship.

Australia:
Men's feelings about divorce:

- 60% proceeded with divorce because their wives wanted to;

- 63% feel dumped;

- 35% will never get over it;

- 33% think divorce was a horrible mistake.

4%
7%

FINLAND
EST
LAT
BELARUS
UKRAINE
REP MOL
ROM
BULG
GREECE
TURKEY
CYPRUS
SYRIA
LEB
ISRAEL
JOR
IRAQ
IRAN
KUWAIT
BAHRAIN
QATAR
UAE
OMAN
YEMEN
EGYPT
SAUDI ARABIA
SUDAN
ERITREA
DJIBOUTI
C A R
ETHIOPIA
SOMALIA
DEM REP CONGO
UGANDA
KENYA
R
B
TANZANIA
SEYCHELLES
COMOROS
ZAMBIA
MALAWI
ZIMBABWE
MADAGASCAR
MAURITIUS
MOZAMBIQUE
BOTSWANA
SOUTH AFRICA
S

GEO
AZER
ARM
KAZAKHSTAN
UZBEKISTAN
TURKMEN
KIRGISTAN
TAJ
AFGHANISTAN
PAKISTAN
MONGOLIA
NEPAL
BHUTAN
B-DESH
BURMA
NORTH KOREA
SOUTH KOREA
TAIWAN
Hong Kong
LAOS
VIETNAM
THAILAND
CAM
PHILIPPINES
SRI LANKA
MALAYSIA
SINGAPORE
BRUNEI
INDONESIA
PAPUA NEW GUINEA

MICRONESIA
KIRIBATI
MARSHALL IS.
NAURU
SOLOMON ISLANDS
TUVALU
VANUATU
NEW CALEDONIA (F)

AUSTRALIA

WESTERN SAMOA
FIJI
FRENCH POLYNESIA (F)
TONGA

NEW ZEALAND

39

Part Three REPRODUCTION

"Avoid conception during times of unusual earthly or heavenly manifestations and on days specified as ill-omened."

— The Tao of Sex,
latter half of Chou Dynasty,
China, about 2,000 years ago

CONTRACEPTION

In some countries almost no-one has access to reliable contraception; in others almost everyone does. It has been estimated that 300 million couples worldwide have no access to family planning services. If their unwanted pregnancies were prevented, world growth rate would fall by 19 percent.

Organizing access to contraception is one problem, but ensuring its effective use is another. Even in countries such as the USA and the UK, where contraception is easily obtainable, more than half of all pregnancies are unplanned. Although the use of contraception is increasing, every day as many as 150,000 unwanted pregnancies are terminated worldwide, one-third of which are performed in unsafe conditions.

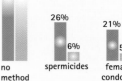

EFFECTIVENESS OF CONTRACEPTIVE METHODS

Percentage of women who become pregnant during the first year of using different methods.

85% 85%
no method

26%
6%
spermicides

21%
5%
female condoms

20%
1%–9%
fertility–aware abstinence

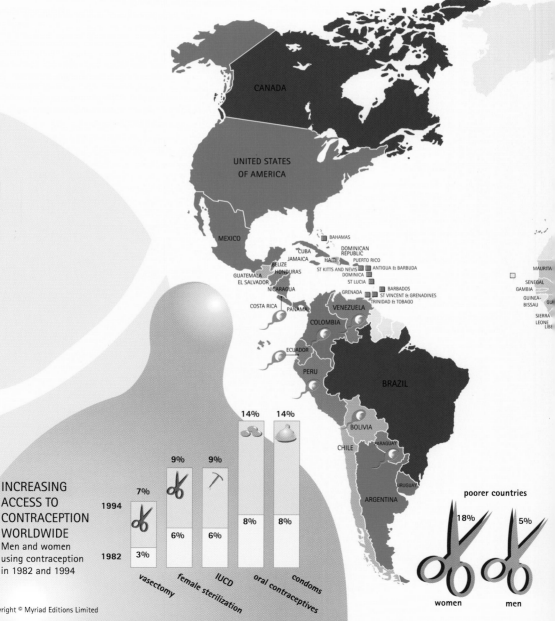

CANADA

UNITED STATES OF AMERICA

MEXICO

BAHAMAS
CUBA
DOMINICAN REPUBLIC
JAMAICA
HAITI
PUERTO RICO
BELIZE
HONDURAS
ST KITTS AND NEVIS
ANTIGUA & BARBUDA
DOMINICA
GUATEMALA
EL SALVADOR
ST LUCIA
NICARAGUA
BARBADOS
GRENADA
ST VINCENT & GRENADINES
TRINIDAD & TOBAGO
COSTA RICA
PANAMA
VENEZUELA

COLOMBIA

ECUADOR

PERU

BRAZIL

BOLIVIA

CHILE
PARAGUAY

URUGUAY

ARGENTINA

MAURITA
SENEGAL
GAMBIA
GUINEA-BISSAU
SIERRA LEONE
LIBE

INCREASING ACCESS TO CONTRACEPTION WORLDWIDE
Men and women using contraception in 1982 and 1994

1994
1982

7%
3%
vasectomy

9%
6%
female sterilization

9%
6%
IUCD

14%
8%
oral contraceptives

14%
8%
condoms

poorer countries

18%
women

5%
men

as commonly used

used correctly and consistently

20%
6%
diaphragm with spermicide

14%
3%
condoms

7%
1%
oral contraception

1% 1%
Norplant implants; vasectomy; injectables; female sterilization; IUCD

TEENAGE ABORTIONS
in Europe

Number of abortions per 1,000 women aged 15 to 19

Bulgaria 45
Romania 43

Hungary 32

UK 20
Norway 19
Sweden 18
Denmark 16
Czech Republic 15
Iceland 14

Finland 9
France 8

Italy 5
Netherlands 4

Germany 2
Greece 2

RUSSIA

NORWAY   FINLAND

DENMARK

NETH
GERMANY
FRANCE
SPAIN

EST
LAT
LIT
BEL
POLAND
CZECH REP
SLOV
HUNG
ROM
YUG
M
ALB
BULG

UKRAINE
MOLDOVA

KAZAKHSTAN

MONGOLIA

NORTH KOREA
JAPAN
SOUTH KOREA

TURKEY
CYPRUS
ISRAEL
GEO
AZER
SYRIA
LEB
JOR
IRAQ

UZBEKISTAN
TURKMEN
KIRGISTAN
TAJ

CHINA

MOROCCO

ALGERIA
LIBYA

IRAN
KUWAIT
BAHRAIN
QATAR
UAE
OMAN

AFGHANISTAN
PAKISTAN

NEPAL
BHUTAN
B-DESH

TAIWAN
Hong Kong SAR

MALI
NIGER
CHAD

EGYPT
SAUDI ARABIA

INDIA
BURMA
LAOS
VIETNAM
CAM
THAILAND

SUDAN
ERITREA
YEMEN
DJIBOUTI

SRI LANKA

PHILIPPINES

BURKINA FASO
GHANA
TOGO
BENIN
NIGERIA
CAR
CAMEROON
CONGO
DEM REP CONGO

ETHIOPIA
SOMALIA
UGANDA
KENYA
R
TANZANIA

BRUNEI
MALAYSIA
SINGAPORE

INDONESIA

PAPUA NEW GUINEA

VANUATU   WESTERN SAMOA
FIJI
NEW CALEDONIA   TONGA   COOK ISLANDS

MARSHALL ISLANDS

KIRIBATI

ANGOLA
ZAMBIA
MALAWI
ZIMBABWE
NAMIBIA
BOTSWANA
SOUTH AFRICA
MOZAMBIQUE

COMOROS

MADAGASCAR
MAURITIUS
REUNION

AUSTRALIA

NEW ZEALAND

USE OF CONTRACEPTION

Percentage of married women using modern contraception: barrier methods, contraceptive pill, implants, injectables, intra-uterine contraceptive devices (IUCD), sterilization

over 70%

50% – 69%

30% – 49%

10% – 29%

less than 10%

no data

10% or more women use traditional methods

richer countries

8%
5%

STERILIZATION
Percentages of men and women sterilized

women   men

43

Each day 120 million acts of sexual intercourse take place, resulting in 910,000 conceptions and 400,000 live births.

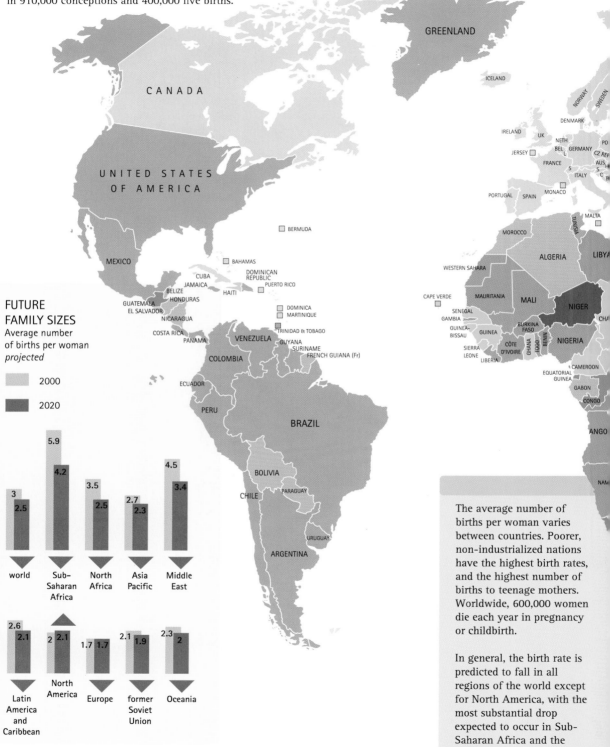

GREENLAND

ICELAND

CANADA

NORWAY
SWEDEN
DENMARK
IRELAND
UK
NETH
PO
JERSEY
BEL
GERMANY
CZ REP
L
AUS
FRANCE
S
ITALY
C
B
MONACO
PORTUGAL
SPAIN

UNITED STATES
OF AMERICA

MALTA
TUNISIA
MOROCCO
ALGERIA
LIBYA
WESTERN SAHARA

BERMUDA

MEXICO
BAHAMAS
CUBA
DOMINICAN
REPUBLIC
JAMAICA
PUERTO RICO
BELIZE
HAITI
HONDURAS
GUATEMALA
EL SALVADOR
NICARAGUA
COSTA RICA
PANAMA

DOMINICA
MARTINIQUE
TRINIDAD & TOBAGO
VENEZUELA
GUYANA
SURINAME
FRENCH GUIANA (Fr)
COLOMBIA

CAPE VERDE
MAURITANIA
MALI
NIGER
CHA
SENEGAL
GAMBIA
GUINEA-
BISSAU
GUINEA
BURKINA
FASO
SIERRA
LEONE
CÔTE
D'IVOIRE
GHANA
TOGO
BENIN
NIGERIA
LIBERIA
CAMEROON
EQUATORIAL
GUINEA
GABON
CONGO

ECUADOR

PERU

BRAZIL

ANGO

BOLIVIA

NAM

PARAGUAY

CHILE

URUGUAY

ARGENTINA

FUTURE FAMILY SIZES

Average number
of births per woman
projected

2000

2020

	world	Sub-Saharan Africa	North Africa	Asia Pacific	Middle East
2000	3	5.9	3.5	2.7	4.5
2020	2.5	4.2	2.5	2.3	3.4

	Latin America and Caribbean	North America	Europe	former Soviet Union	Oceania
2000	2.6	2	1.7	2.1	2.3
2020	2.1	2.1	1.7	1.9	2

The average number of births per woman varies between countries. Poorer, non-industrialized nations have the highest birth rates, and the highest number of births to teenage mothers. Worldwide, 600,000 women die each year in pregnancy or childbirth.

In general, the birth rate is predicted to fall in all regions of the world except for North America, with the most substantial drop expected to occur in Sub-Saharan Africa and the Middle East.

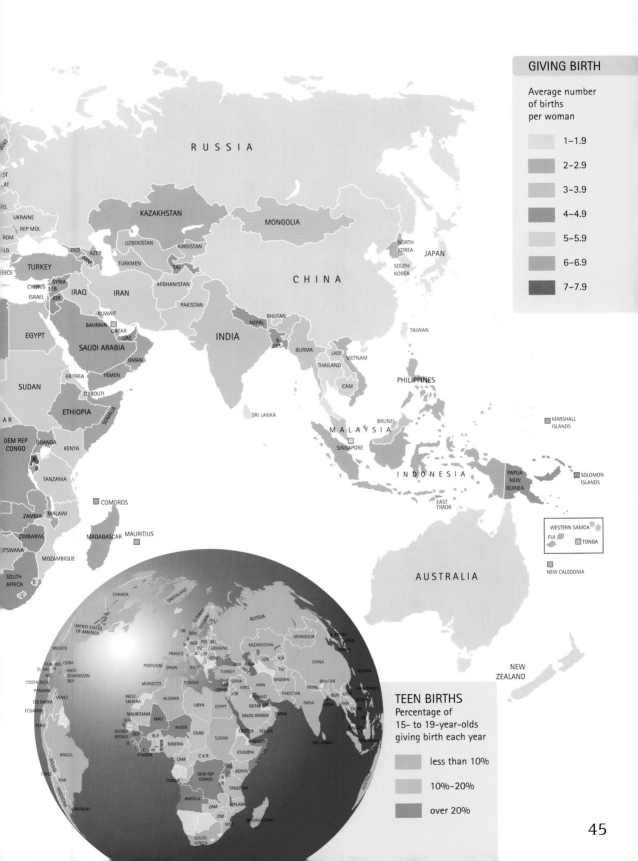

GIVING BIRTH

Average number
of births
per woman

	1–1.9
	2–2.9
	3–3.9
	4–4.9
	5–5.9
	6–6.9
	7–7.9

RUSSIA

KAZAKHSTAN

MONGOLIA

NORTH
KOREA

JAPAN

UZBEKISTAN

KIRGISTAN

SOUTH
KOREA

TURKMEN

TAJ

CHINA

AFGHANISTAN

TURKEY

CYPRUS
SYRIA LEB
ISRAEL JOR
IRAQ

IRAN

PAKISTAN

TAIWAN

KUWAIT

BAHRAIN
QATAR
UAE

NEPAL

BHUTAN

EGYPT

SAUDI ARABIA

INDIA

B-
DESH

BURMA

OMAN

LAOS

VIETNAM

THAILAND

ERITREA
YEMEN

SUDAN

DJIBOUTI

CAM

PHILIPPINES

ETHIOPIA

SOMALIA

SRI LANKA

BRUNEI

MARSHALL
ISLANDS

DEM REP
CONGO

UGANDA

KENYA

MALAYSIA

SINGAPORE

TANZANIA

INDONESIA

PAPUA
NEW
GUINEA

SOLOMON
ISLANDS

COMOROS

EAST
TIMOR

ZAMBIA

MALAWI

ZIMBABWE

MADAGASCAR MAURITIUS

WESTERN SAMOA

FIJI

TONGA

OTSWANA

MOZAMBIQUE

NEW CALEDONIA

SOUTH
AFRICA

AUSTRALIA

NEW
ZEALAND

TEEN BIRTHS
Percentage of
15- to 19-year-olds
giving birth each year

	less than 10%
	10%–20%
	over 20%

CANADA

GREENLAND

UNITED STATES
OF AMERICA

RUSSIA

MONGOLIA

MEXICO

KAZAKHSTAN

CHINA

PORTUGAL SPAIN

TURKEY

SYRIA
IRAQ IRAN

AFGHAN

PAKISTAN

GUA BEL CUBA
EL SAL
NIC HAITI DOMINICAN
COSTA RICA REP
PANAMA

MOROCCO

TUNISIA

NEPAL
BHUTAN

BUR

COLOMBIA VENEZ
ECUADOR

WEST.
SAHARA

ALGERIA

LIBYA

EGYPT

SAUDI
ARABIA

QATAR UAE
OMAN

INDIA

B-
DESH

THAI

PERU

MAURITANIA

MALI

NIGER

CHAD

SUDAN

ERITREA YEMEN

SRI LANKA

BRAZIL

GUINEA
BISSAU

SEN
G
SL

GUI

B-F

NIGERIA

D'IVOIRE

CAM

C A R

ETHIOPIA

DJIBOUTI

SOMALIA

BOLIVIA

CHILE

PAR

ANGOLA

DEM REP
CONGO

CONGO

KENYA

TANZANIA

ZAM

MALAWI

MADAGASCAR

ARGENTINA

URUGUAY

ZIM

MOZ

SOUTH
AFRICA

INFERTILITY

Worldwide, 70 million couples are infertile. Infertility in men amounts to 40 percent of the total.

CANADA

UNITED STATES OF AMERICA

MEXICO

CUBA
JAMAICA
DOMINICAN REPUBLIC
BELIZE
HAITI
HONDURAS
GUATEMALA
EL SALVADOR
NICARAGUA
COSTA RICA
PANAMA

VENEZUELA
COLOMBIA
ECUADOR
PERU
BRAZIL
BOLIVIA
PARAGUAY
CHILE
URUGUAY
ARGENTINA

A study of infertile men in Italy showed that their sperm count was at its highest at around 5 o'clock in the afternoon.

NORWAY
SWEDEN
FIN
DENMARK
UK
NETH
BEL
GERMANY
POLAND
FRANCE
CZ REP
AUS
HUN
S
ITALY
YU
PORTUGAL
SPAIN
ALB

MOROCCO
TUNISIA
ALGERIA
LIBYA

MAURITANIA
MALI
NIGER
CHA
SENEGAL
GUINEA
BURKINA FASO
SIERRA LEONE
CÔTE D'IVOIRE
GHANA
TOGO
BENIN
NIGERIA
LIBERIA
CAMEROON
C A

CONGO
DEM CON

ANGOLA

SOU
AFRI

HEAT EXHAUSTION

The sperm concentration of outdoor workers in Texas, USA was 32% lower in summer than in winter.

Many of the causes of infertility remain a mystery, but some factors are known, such as complications following childbirth or abortion, sexually-transmitted infections (STIs), and the use of alcohol and tobacco. Fertility rates of women who smoke are 30 percent lower than those of non-smokers. Tobacco can also lead to malformed sperm and impotence in men. High infertility rates in Central Africa relate to the high incidence of STIs.

Proportion of couples with primary infertility

- 2%–4%
- 5%–9%
- 10%–14%
- 15%–19%
- 20% and over

no data

MONGOLIA

NORTH KOREA

JAPAN

C H I N A

SOUTH KOREA

TURKEY

CYPRUS

SYRIA
LEB

ISRAEL
JOR

IRAQ

IRAN

AFGHANISTAN

PAKISTAN

TAIWAN

HONG KONG

KUWAIT

BHUTAN

NEPAL

EGYPT

SAUDI ARABIA

OMAN

YEMEN

INDIA

B. DESH

BURMA

LAOS

VIETNAM

THAILAND

PHILIPPINES

SUDAN

CAM

ETHIOPIA

SOMALIA

SRI LANKA

BRUNEI

UGANDA

KENYA

R
B

MALAYSIA

SINGAPORE

INDONESIA

PAPUA NEW GUINEA

TANZANIA

ZAMBIA

MALAWI

ZIMBABWE

MADAGASCAR

MOZAMBIQUE

AUSTRALIA

ALCOHOL IMPEDES PREGNANCY
Percentage of women in Denmark, with different weekly alcohol consumptions, becoming pregnant within six months of discontinuing contraception.

Fewer than five drinks 64%

More than ten drinks 55%

NEW ZEALAND

47

CLONING

Cloning will further separate sex from procreation. It will allow heterosexuals, the infertile, singles, gays, lesbians and transgender people to have a child without heterosexual sex. Full human cloning is inevitable, though the timetable remains vague.

☐ ICELAND

NORWAY

1997 sheep
SCOTLAND

SWEDEN

DENMARK

IRELAND   UK

NETH   POLAND

France 1999:
Warning of
long-term
health defects.

BEL

GERMANY   CZ REP

SLOV

FRANCE   SWITZ   AUSTRIA   HUNGARY

ITALY

SPAIN

CANADA

UNITED STATES
OF AMERICA

USA 1997:
Raelian religious
movement
announces it will
clone children, and
that life on earth
was started by
aliens cloning
humans in a
laboratory.

USA 1997:
Jesuit priest
proclaims cloned
human would
have a different
soul.

USA 1994–97:
Early experimentation
in cloning human
embryo

MEXICO

USA 1998:
cloning mice

BRAZIL

ARGENTINA

SOUT
AFRI

PUBLIC OPINION
in the USA

89% say human cloning is morally unacceptable
66% say animal cloning is morally unacceptable
69% are scared of the possibility of human cloning
74% say human cloning is against God's will
19% say human cloning is not against God's will

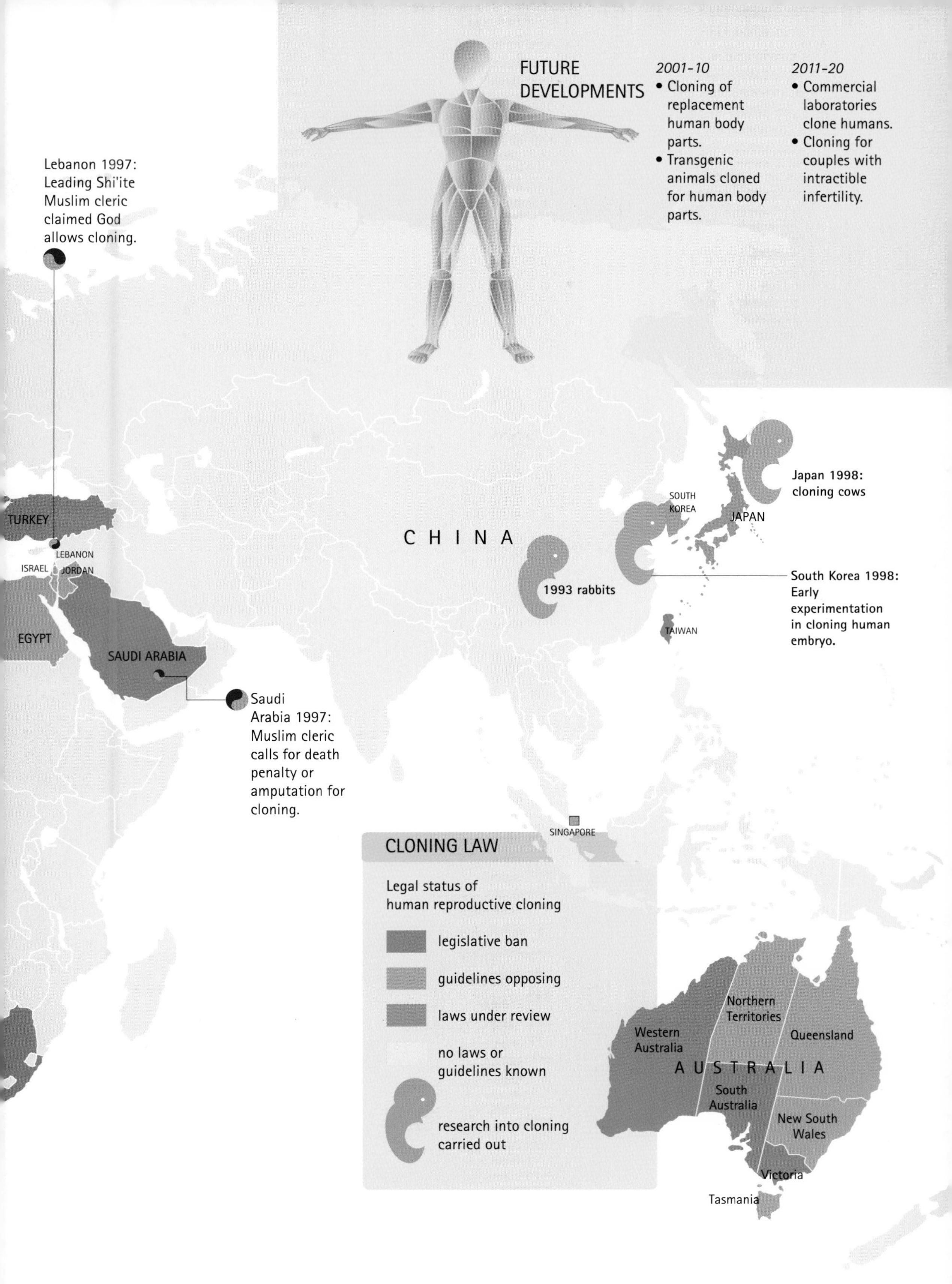

FUTURE DEVELOPMENTS

2001-10
- Cloning of replacement human body parts.
- Transgenic animals cloned for human body parts.

2011-20
- Commercial laboratories clone humans.
- Cloning for couples with intractible infertility.

Lebanon 1997: Leading Shi'ite Muslim cleric claimed God allows cloning.

TURKEY

LEBANON

ISRAEL   JORDAN

EGYPT

SAUDI ARABIA

Saudi Arabia 1997: Muslim cleric calls for death penalty or amputation for cloning.

C H I N A

SOUTH KOREA

JAPAN

Japan 1998: cloning cows

1993 rabbits

South Korea 1998: Early experimentation in cloning human embryo.

TAIWAN

SINGAPORE

CLONING LAW

Legal status of human reproductive cloning

- legislative ban
- guidelines opposing
- laws under review
- no laws or guidelines known
- research into cloning carried out

AUSTRALIA

Western Australia

Northern Territories

Queensland

South Australia

New South Wales

Victoria

Tasmania

49

Part Four SEXUAL HEALTH

"Sexual health is far more than freedom from diseases.
It encompasses the capacity to derive pleasure from sex.
Sexual health is a basic human right."

— Eli Coleman,
President, World Congress of Sexology,
Hong Kong,1999

SEX EDUCATION

Finding out about sex is often hindered by laws, regulations, policies, and public opposition – to sex education in schools, to disseminating sex and family planning information, to advertising, displaying and providing contraceptives, and by censorship laws governing obscenity. Good sexual practices end up being discovered, often in a haphazard manner, rather than taught.

What information young people glean comes primarily from their friends, school, books, sex partners, and parents. Since the mid-1990s, the BBC World Service has broadcast sex programs in a number of languages around the world. The internet is a more recent source of information for many, with sites that provide information and answer questions about love, relationships, and sex.

after sex education in the USA

GOING DOWN

- Fewer young people initiated sex.
- Pregnancy rates fell by 30%.
- Abortion rate fell.

FIRST SEX EDUCATION
Average age of children receiving sex education

Germany	UK	Canada, Italy	Spain	Mexico	France, USA	Czech Republic	Poland	Greece	Taiwan	Singapore, Thailand
11.3	11.4	11.5	11.7	11.9	12.0	12.5	12.7	12.9	13.0	13.5

Although the average age for first sex education is 12.2 years, 58% of adults believe sex education should start before the age of 12.

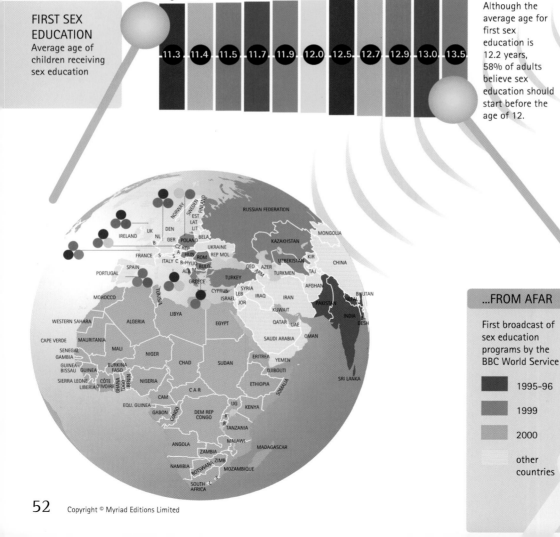

...FROM AFAR

First broadcast of sex education programs by the BBC World Service

- 1995-96
- 1999
- 2000
- other countries

GOING UP

after sex education in the USA

- Average age of first intercourse rose by 7 months.
- Attendance at family planning clinics increased by 70%.
- Percentage of girls using contraception increased from 37% to 50%.

USA 1994: Surgeon General dismissed for suggesting masturbation be taught in schools, as part of human sexuality.

Malaysia: Family planning authorities found that at least 2% of couples seeking fertility treatment are ignorant of sex and have not consummated their marriages.

KNOWLEDGE OF SEX
in the Philippines

Percentage of women aged 15 to 50

very knowledgeable — 6%

not at all knowledgeable 32%

some knowledge 18%

fairly knowledgeable 45%

...FROM CLOSE BY

Main sources of finding out about sex

- parents
- sexual partners
- friends
- books
- taught at school

53

SAFER SEX

Safe sex means having sex only with a partner who has never had another partner. Safer sex means reducing the number of sex partners, avoiding sex when one parter has a sexually-transmitted infection (STI), promptly treating all STIs, and avoiding skin contact or exchange of bodily fluids from the penis, vagina, mouth, and anus.

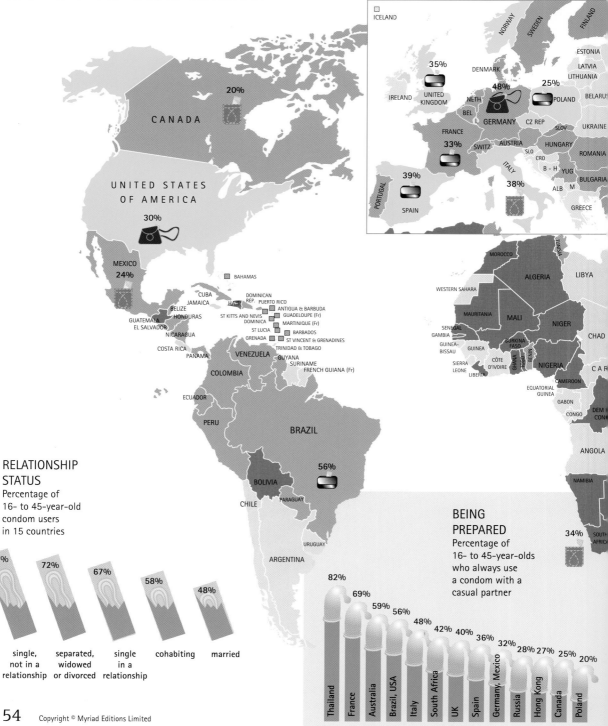

RELATIONSHIP STATUS
Percentage of 16- to 45-year-old condom users in 15 countries

- 77% single, not in a relationship
- 72% separated, widowed or divorced
- 67% single in a relationship
- 58% cohabiting
- 48% married

BEING PREPARED
Percentage of 16- to 45-year-olds who always use a condom with a casual partner

- 82% Thailand
- 69% France
- 59% Australia
- 56% Brazil, USA
- 48% Italy
- 42% South Africa
- 40% UK
- 36% Spain
- 32% Germany, Mexico
- 28% Russia
- 27% Hong Kong
- 25% Canada
- 20% Poland
- 34% South Africa

Map labels

CANADA 20%
UNITED STATES OF AMERICA 30%
MEXICO 24%
BRAZIL 56%

UNITED KINGDOM 35%
GERMANY 48%
POLAND 25%
FRANCE 33%
SPAIN 39%
ITALY 38%

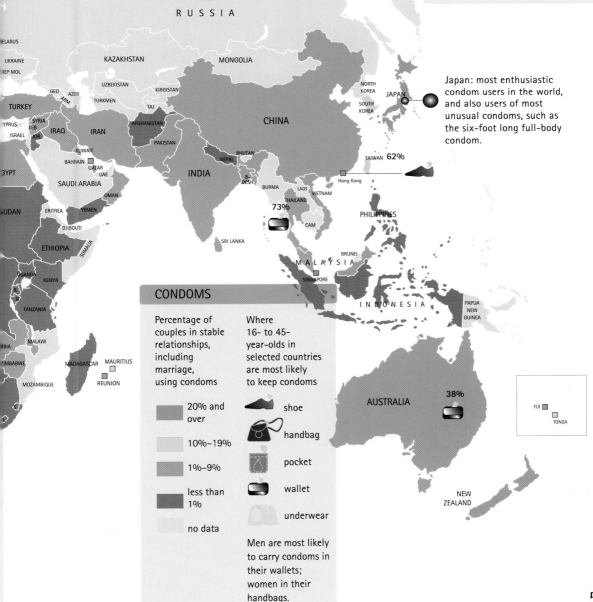

The emergence of AIDS in the 1980s added impetus to the need to practice safer sex. One way is by using a condom during penetrative sexual intercourse and oro-genital sex. Yet, worldwide, only 5 percent of couples use condoms: 14 percent in rich countries and 3 percent in poor countries.

44%

RUSSIA

Japan: most enthusiastic condom users in the world, and also users of most unusual condoms, such as the six-foot long full-body condom.

BELARUS
UKRAINE
REP MOL
KAZAKHSTAN
MONGOLIA
UZBEKISTAN
KIRGISTAN
NORTH KOREA
JAPAN
GEO
AZER
ARM
TURKMEN
TAJ
SOUTH KOREA
TURKEY
CYPRUS
SYRIA
LEB
ISRAEL
JOR
IRAQ
IRAN
AFGHANISTAN
PAKISTAN
CHINA
KUWAIT
BAHRAIN
QATAR
UAE
TAIWAN 62%
EGYPT
SAUDI ARABIA
OMAN
INDIA
BHUTAN
NEPAL
B-DESH
Hong Kong
SUDAN
ERITREA
YEMEN
BURMA
LAOS
VIETNAM
THAILAND
DJIBOUTI
SOMALIA
73%
CAM
PHILIPPINES
ETHIOPIA
SRI LANKA
UGANDA
KENYA
BRUNEI
MALAYSIA
TANZANIA
SINGAPORE
INDONESIA
PAPUA NEW GUINEA
ZAMBIA
MALAWI
ZIMBABWE
MADAGASCAR
MAURITIUS
MOZAMBIQUE
REUNION

CONDOMS

Percentage of couples in stable relationships, including marriage, using condoms

Where 16- to 45-year-olds in selected countries are most likely to keep condoms

20% and over	shoe
10%–19%	handbag
1%–9%	pocket
less than 1%	wallet
no data	underwear

Men are most likely to carry condoms in their wallets; women in their handbags.

AUSTRALIA
38%

FIJI
TONGA

NEW ZEALAND

55

SEXUALLY-TRANSMITTED INFECTIONS

Each day, over a million people contract a sexually-transmitted infection (STI) — an historical and ever-present hazard of sexual contact. Initially incurable STIs continually emerge, such as syphilis, gonorrhea, herpes and, most recently, acquired immune deficiency syndrome (AIDS). New infections will emerge in the 21st century.

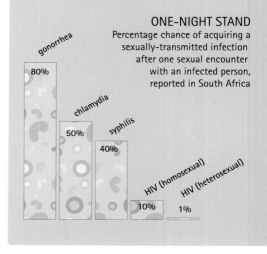

ONE-NIGHT STAND
Percentage chance of acquiring a sexually-transmitted infection after one sexual encounter with an infected person, reported in South Africa

gonorrhea 80%
chlamydia 50%
syphilis 40%
HIV (homosexual) 10%
HIV (heterosexual) 1%

ANATOMY OF AN EPIDEMIC
Millions of people affected by HIV / AIDS

- men
- women
- children

deaths from AIDS in 1998
0.5 million
0.9 million
1.1 million

people newly-infected with HIV in 1998
0.6 million
2.1 million
3.1 million

people living with HIV / AIDS in 1998
18.4 million
13.8 million
1.2 million

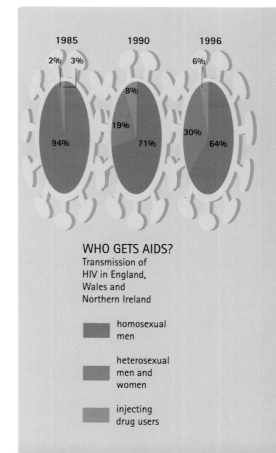

1985 · 2% · 3% · 94%
1990 · 8% · 19% · 71%
1996 · 6% · 30% · 64%

WHO GETS AIDS?
Transmission of HIV in England, Wales and Northern Ireland

- homosexual men
- heterosexual men and women
- injecting drug users

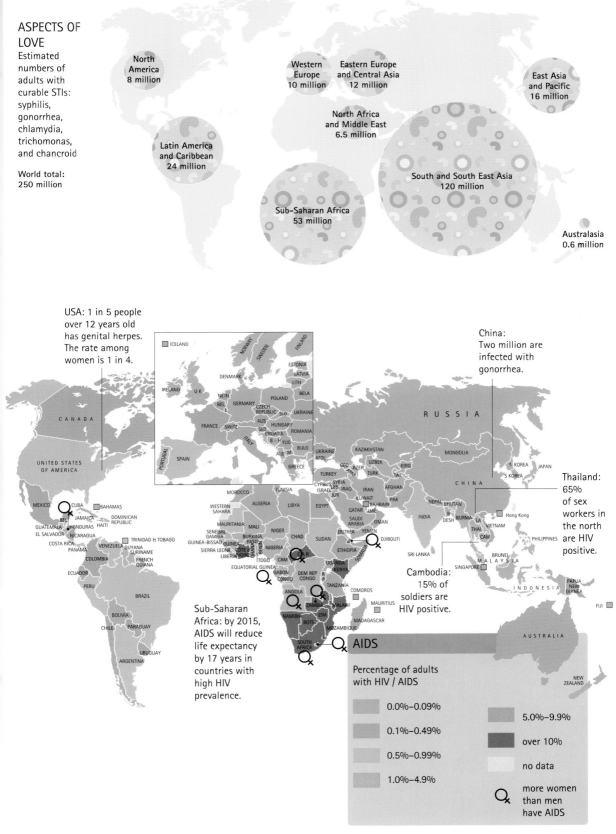

ASPECTS OF LOVE

Estimated numbers of adults with curable STIs: syphilis, gonorrhea, chlamydia, trichomonas, and chancroid

World total: 250 million

North America
8 million

Western Europe
10 million

Eastern Europe and Central Asia
12 million

East Asia and Pacific
16 million

North Africa and Middle East
6.5 million

Latin America and Caribbean
24 million

South and South East Asia
120 million

Sub-Saharan Africa
53 million

Australasia
0.6 million

USA: 1 in 5 people over 12 years old has genital herpes. The rate among women is 1 in 4.

China: Two million are infected with gonorrhea.

Thailand: 65% of sex workers in the north are HIV positive.

Cambodia: 15% of soldiers are HIV positive.

Sub-Saharan Africa: by 2015, AIDS will reduce life expectancy by 17 years in countries with high HIV prevalence.

AIDS

Percentage of adults with HIV / AIDS

- 0.0%–0.09%
- 0.1%–0.49%
- 0.5%–0.99%
- 1.0%–4.9%
- 5.0%–9.9%
- over 10%
- no data

Qₓ more women than men have AIDS

ICELAND

NORWAY · SWEDEN · FINLAND

DENMARK · ESTONIA · LATVIA · LITH

IRELAND · UK · NETH · BEL · GERMANY · POLAND · BELA

FRANCE · SWITZ · CZECH REPUBLIC · SLO · AUS · HUNGARY · UKRAINE

PORTUGAL · SPAIN · ITALY · SLO · CROATIA · B-H · YUG · ROMANIA · MOL

ALB · MAC · BULG · UKRAINE

GREECE

CANADA

UNITED STATES OF AMERICA

MEXICO · CUBA · BAHAMAS
BEL · JAMAICA · DOMINICAN REPUBLIC
GUATEMALA · HONDURAS · HAITI
EL SALVADOR · NICARAGUA
COSTA RICA · TRINIDAD & TOBAGO
PANAMA · VENEZUELA · GUYANA · SURINAME
COLOMBIA · FRENCH GUIANA
ECUADOR
PERU
BRAZIL
BOLIVIA
PARAGUAY
CHILE
URUGUAY
ARGENTINA

MOROCCO · TUNISIA
WESTERN SAHARA · ALGERIA · LIBYA · EGYPT
MAURITANIA · MALI · NIGER · CHAD · SUDAN · ERITREA · YEMEN · DJIBOUTI
SENEGAL · GAMBIA · BURKINA FASO
GUINEA-BISSAU · GUINEA · NIGERIA · ETHIOPIA · SOMALIA
SIERRA LEONE · COTE D'IVOIRE · GHANA · BENIN · CAR
LIBERIA · TOGO · CAM · UGANDA · KENYA
EQUATORIAL GUINEA · GABON · CONGO · DEM REP CONGO · RB
ANGOLA · TANZANIA · COMOROS
ZAMBIA · MALAWI · MAURITIUS
NAMIBIA · BOTS · MOZAMBIQUE · MADAGASCAR
SOUTH AFRICA

TURKEY · GEO · AZER · UZBEK · KIRG
CYPRUS · SYRIA · ARM · TURK · TAJ
ISRAEL · LEB · IRAQ · IRAN · AFGHAN
JOR · KUWAIT · PAK
QATAR · UAE · SAUDI ARABIA · OMAN
NEPAL · BHUTAN
INDIA · DESH · BURMA · LA · VIETNAM
SRI LANKA · THAI · CAM · PHILIPPINES
SINGAPORE · BRUNEI · MALAYSIA
INDONESIA

KAZAKHSTAN

RUSSIA

MONGOLIA

N KOREA · JAPAN
S KOREA
CHINA
Hong Kong

PAPUA NEW GUINEA
FIJI

AUSTRALIA

NEW ZEALAND

57

COUNSELING

Most sexual problems can be treated successfully.

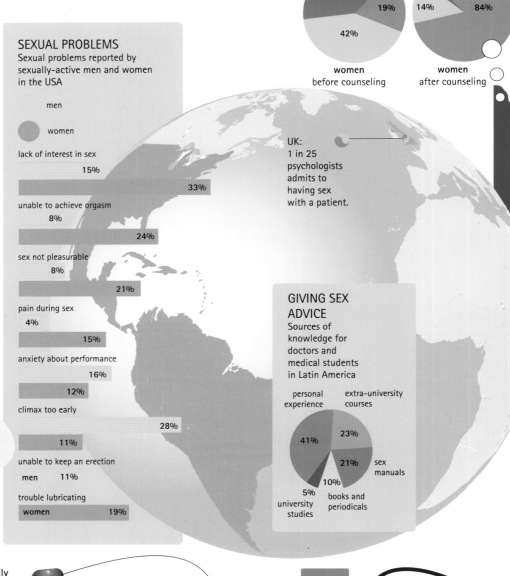

women
before counseling

39%
19%
42%

women
after counseling

2%
14%
84%

SEXUAL PROBLEMS
Sexual problems reported by
sexually-active men and women
in the USA

men

women

lack of interest in sex
15%
33%

unable to achieve orgasm
8%
24%

sex not pleasurable
8%
21%

pain during sex
4%
15%

anxiety about performance
16%
12%

climax too early
28%
11%

unable to keep an erection
men   11%

trouble lubricating
women   19%

UK:
1 in 25
psychologists
admits to
having sex
with a patient.

GIVING SEX ADVICE
Sources of
knowledge for
doctors and
medical students
in Latin America

personal
experience   41%

extra-university
courses   23%

sex
manuals   21%

books and
periodicals   10%

university
studies   5%

**topics occasionally
asked about:**
circumcision
female ejaculation
homosexual sex
during menstruation
odors
painful sex
pleasing a partner
rape / abuse
urinating during sex
vagina shape
vaginal fisting
vasectomy

**topics frequently
asked about:**
oral sex
pubic hair
fantasies / role playing
three- and foursomes
penis size
phone / internet sex
sex toys
first sex
birth control
vaginal control

**topics most
frequently
asked about:**
masturbation
orgasm
anatomy
impotence
lack of desire
STIs
anal sex

FAQs...
Topics for
questions
about sex
asked on
the internet

... AND WHO ASKS THEM

men
66%

women
34%

39%

39%

22%

men
before counseling

3%

23% 74%

men
after counseling

SEXUAL SATISFACTION
Degree of sexual satisfaction
before and after counseling
reported by men and women in the UK

- no enjoyment
- some enjoyment
- enjoyment on most occasions

SUCCESSFUL COUNSELING
Proportion of sexual problems in the UK
that improved after counseling

vaginal pain on penile entry	80%
women's enjoyment of sex	75%
premature ejaculation	74%
women's interest and arousal	71%
getting erections	66%
delayed ejaculation	55%
men's enjoyment	53%
problems having an orgasm	49%

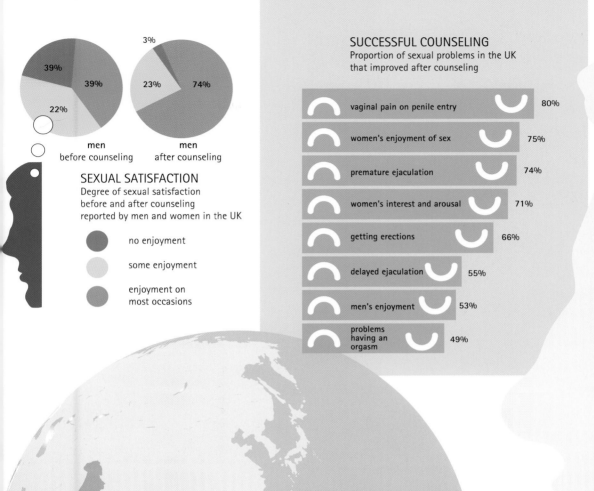

SEXUAL PROBLEMS

Problems
presented by
men aged 21 to 30
attending
psychosexual
clinics in India

no
sexual
contact
10%

fear
of STI
13%

abnormal
sensation
in genitals
14%

worry
about
nocturnal
emissions
20%

erectile
dysfunction
24%

small
penis
30%

guilt
about
masturbation
33%

nocturnal
emissions
71%

premature
ejaculation
78%

59

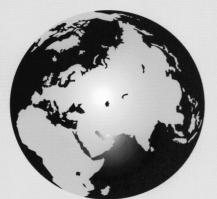

Part Five THE BUSINESS OF SEX

"Only two things always sell well: food and sex.
And I was never much of a cook."

– Fernande Grudet ("Madame Claude")
head of France's biggest prostitution ring
in the 1960s and 1970s

THE ECONOMICS OF SEX

Sex is worth billions of dollars and creates millions of jobs.

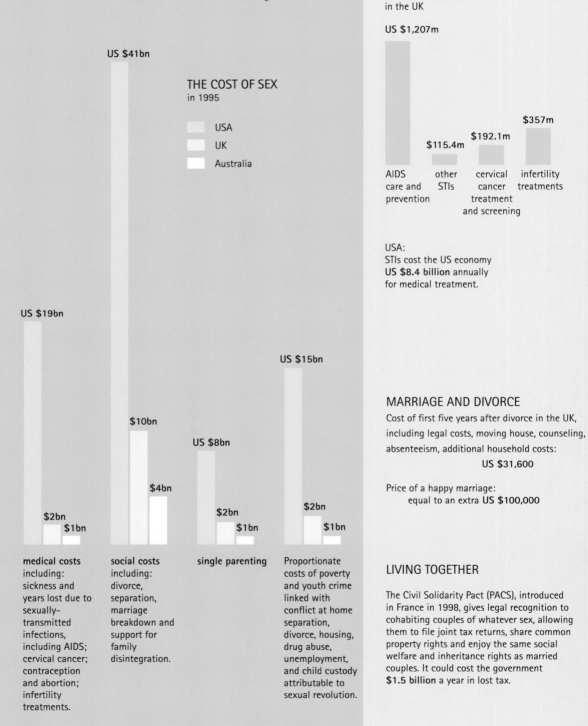

THE COST OF SEX
in 1995

- USA
- UK
- Australia

US $41bn

US $19bn

US $15bn

$10bn

US $8bn

$4bn

$2bn
$1bn

$2bn
$1bn

$2bn
$1bn

medical costs including: sickness and years lost due to sexually-transmitted infections, including AIDS; cervical cancer; contraception and abortion; infertility treatments.

social costs including: divorce, separation, marriage breakdown and support for family disintegration.

single parenting

Proportionate costs of poverty and youth crime linked with conflict at home separation, divorce, housing, drug abuse, unemployment, and child custody attributable to sexual revolution.

ANNUAL HEALTH CARE COSTS
in the UK

US $1,207m

$115.4m

$192.1m

$357m

AIDS care and prevention

other STIs

cervical cancer treatment and screening

infertility treatments

USA:
STIs cost the US economy **US $8.4 billion** annually for medical treatment.

MARRIAGE AND DIVORCE

Cost of first five years after divorce in the UK, including legal costs, moving house, counseling, absenteeism, additional household costs:
US $31,600

Price of a happy marriage:
equal to an extra **US $100,000**

LIVING TOGETHER

The Civil Solidarity Pact (PACS), introduced in France in 1998, gives legal recognition to cohabiting couples of whatever sex, allowing them to file joint tax returns, share common property rights and enjoy the same social welfare and inheritance rights as married couples. It could cost the government **$1.5 billion** a year in lost tax.

PROSTITUTION

Internet prostitution:
In 1997, the annual income from the online sex industry in the USA was estimated at **US $1 billion.**

Thailand:
prostitution generates an annual income of **US $25 billion, $300 million** of which is transferred to rural families by women working in the urban sex industry.

Taiwan:
US $2 billion is spent on paid sex.

Indonesia:
Annual turnover of the sex industry is **US $3.3 billion.**

Australia:
Melbourne has over 70 legal brothels, the largest of which has an annual turnover of **US $1.4 million.**

Tuvalu:
In the global telephone sex network, calls to New Zealand from the UK, USA and Japan are frequently routed via Tuvalu, contributing **10%** of the country's annual revenue.

TAIWAN

THAILAND

INDONESIA

TUVALU

AUSTRALIA

NEW ZEALAND

SEX CRIME

Rape is the costliest crime. With annual victim costs totalling **US $127 billion** in the USA, it exacts a higher price than murder.

$127bn	$93bn	$71bn	$61bn	$56bn
rape	assault	murder	drink driving	child abuse

Economic costs to the victim: tangible, out-of-pocket costs, including medical and mental health care: **US $5,100**

HOMOSEXUALITY

Annual spending power of lesbian and gay market in Australia: **US $30 billion**

Annual gay festival in Sydney injects **US $23 million** into the economy.

PORNOGRAPHY

In 1996, the internet hosted over 600 commercial pornography sites, generating revenues of over **US $51 million.**

By 2000, some porn sites generated **US $20 million** annually.

Online sex industry generates **US $1 billion** per year.

After drugs and gambling, pornography is the most profitable organised crime industry.

SAFER SEX

In 1999, Durex condom sales were in excess of **US $224 million.**

SEX ENHANCEMENT

Viagra worldwide sales:

US $1 billion

$750 million

$350 million

| 1998 | 1999 | 2000 |

PORNOGRAPHY

The USA is the world's leading producer and consumer of pornography.

Most users of pornography are young men. Men's use of pornography has been compared with women's consumption of romantic novels, both using fantasy to compensate for a disappointing reality.

Measuring the impact of pornography is difficult. There is no universally accepted definition of pornography. Research into its effects has produced mixed results, but little evidence that adult, non-violent pornography leads to sex offences. In contrast, "slasher" films that fuse sex with violence have been shown to reduce sensitivity towards rape victims and increase acceptance of the use of sexual force.

Humans have always been fascinated by the sight of other humans having sex. The Chinese Yellow Emperor Shih Huang-Ti chronicled Taoist sex positions in 200 BC; Vatsyayana's *Kama Sutra* in the 3rd century AD is regarded as an Indian classic on the art of lovemaking, spawning erotic sculptures and illustrations through the ages. In Europe, printed pornography began with the art works of Raimondi and Romano in the 1520s, showing explicit scenes of sexual intercourse. Today, the internet has moved pornography into the home.

Thousands of children worldwide are made use of to produce child pornography. The United Nations' Convention on the Rights of the Child identifies child pornography as a violation against children, and requires nations to take measures to prevent the exploitative use of children in pornographic materials.

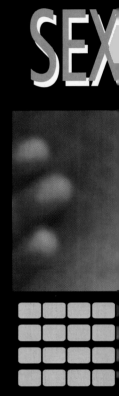

ATTITUDES TO PORNOGRAPHY
Percentages in Finland supporting 16-year olds buying porn at licensed stores

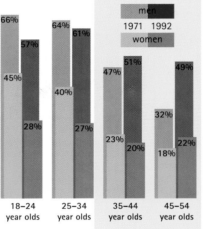

men
1971 1992
women

	18–24 year olds	25–34 year olds	35–44 year olds	45–54 year olds
men 1971	45%	40%	23%	18%
men 1992	66%	64%	47%	32%
women 1971	28%	27%	20%	22%
women 1992	57%	61%	51%	49%

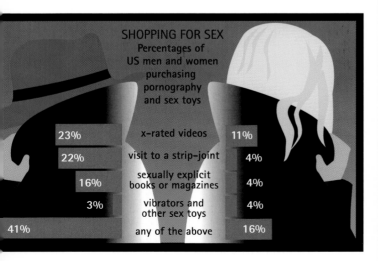

SHOPPING FOR SEX
Percentages of US men and women purchasing pornography and sex toys

	men	women
x-rated videos	23%	11%
visit to a strip-joint	22%	4%
sexually explicit books or magazines	16%	4%
vibrators and other sex toys	3%	4%
any of the above	41%	16%

CENSORSHIP

All countries, to a varying degree, censor nudity, pornography, pedophilia, and sex acts in public. Many have laws banning "lewd", "indecent", or "obscene" materials. Attitudes towards erotica, pornography, obscenity, and even sex education have fluctuated through the ages, and vary from country to country. Censorship laws and regulations that do exist may not be enforced. The current global trend is towards liberalization, with backlashes in some countries.

Censorship poses the policy dilemma of consumer protection, regulation, and social control versus consumer choice, freedom, self-determination, and personal responsibility. Some believe that pornography is a small price to pay for defending freedom of speech, but are uncomfortable with sexual violence, pedophilia or pornography being universally available, especially to children.

ONLINE

CANADA 4.3%

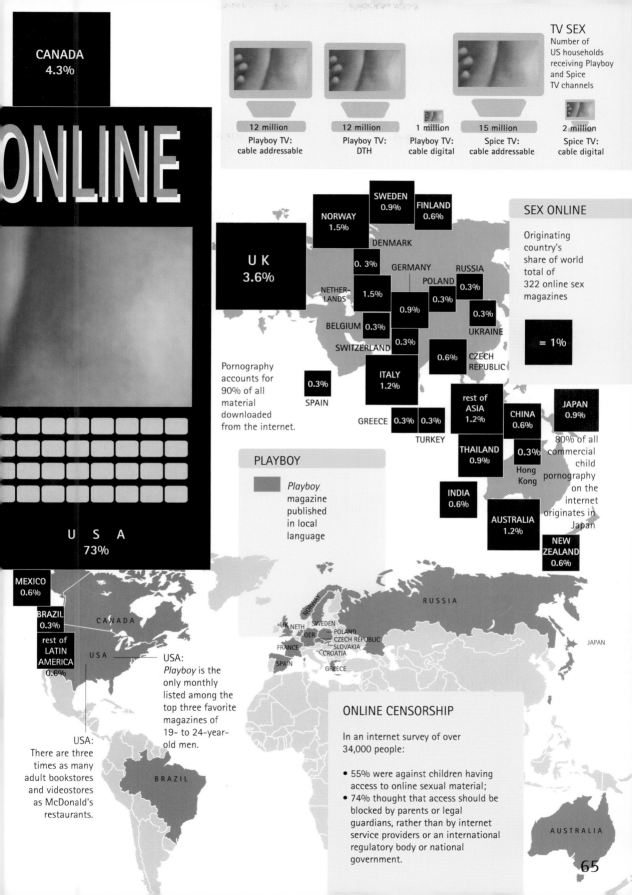

TV SEX
Number of US households receiving Playboy and Spice TV channels

12 million	12 million	1 million	15 million	2 million
Playboy TV: cable addressable	Playboy TV: DTH	Playboy TV: cable digital	Spice TV: cable addressable	Spice TV: cable digital

SEX ONLINE

Originating country's share of world total of 322 online sex magazines

= 1%

U K 3.6%

SWEDEN 0.9%

FINLAND 0.6%

NORWAY 1.5%

DENMARK 0.3%

GERMANY

RUSSIA

POLAND 0.3%

NETHER-LANDS 1.5%

0.9%

0.3%

UKRAINE 0.3%

BELGIUM 0.3%

SWITZERLAND 0.3%

0.6%

CZECH REPUBLIC

Pornography accounts for 90% of all material downloaded from the internet.

0.3%
SPAIN

ITALY 1.2%

rest of ASIA 1.2%

CHINA 0.6%

JAPAN 0.9%

GREECE 0.3% | 0.3%
TURKEY

THAILAND 0.9%

0.3%
Hong Kong

80% of all commercial child pornography on the internet originates in Japan

INDIA 0.6%

AUSTRALIA 1.2%

NEW ZEALAND 0.6%

PLAYBOY

Playboy magazine published in local language

MEXICO 0.6%

BRAZIL 0.3%

rest of LATIN AMERICA 0.6%

USA:
Playboy is the only monthly listed among the top three favorite magazines of 19- to 24-year-old men.

USA:
There are three times as many adult bookstores and videostores as McDonald's restaurants.

USA 73%

ONLINE CENSORSHIP

In an internet survey of over 34,000 people:

- 55% were against children having access to online sexual material;
- 74% thought that access should be blocked by parents or legal guardians, rather than by internet service providers or an international regulatory body or national government.

65

PROSTITUTION

In the last hundred years, prostitution has developed into a huge international business, fuelled by wars, poverty, migration, dreams, hopes, and despair. Many countries have decriminalized prostitution, but other activities, such as soliciting, pimping, and advertising sexual services, often remain a criminal offence.

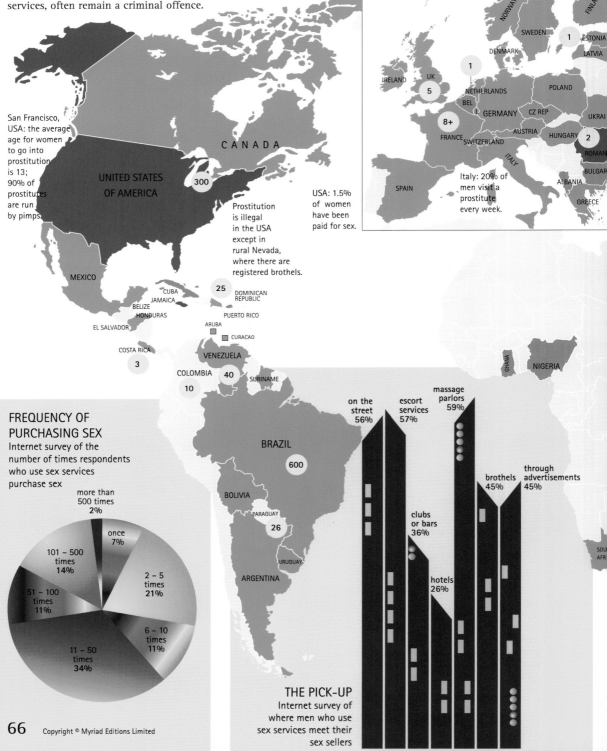

ICELAND

NORWAY
SWEDEN
FINLAND
DENMARK
IRELAND
UK **5**
NETHERLANDS
BEL
GERMANY
POLAND
1
ESTONIA
LATVIA
FRANCE **8+**
SWITZERLAND
AUSTRIA
CZ REP
UKRAI
HUNGARY **2**
ITALY
ROMANI
SPAIN
ALBANIA
BULGAR
GREECE

Italy: 20% of men visit a prostitute every week.

San Francisco, USA: the average age for women to go into prostitution is 13; 90% of prostitutes are run by pimps.

CANADA

UNITED STATES OF AMERICA **300**

Prostitution is illegal in the USA except in rural Nevada, where there are registered brothels.

USA: 1.5% of women have been paid for sex.

MEXICO

CUBA
JAMAICA
BELIZE
HONDURAS
EL SALVADOR

DOMINICAN REPUBLIC **25**

PUERTO RICO
ARUBA
CURACAO

COSTA RICA **3**

VENEZUELA **40**
COLOMBIA **10**
SURINAME

GHANA
NIGERIA

BRAZIL **600**

BOLIVIA
PARAGUAY **26**
URUGUAY
ARGENTINA

SOU
AFR

FREQUENCY OF PURCHASING SEX

Internet survey of the number of times respondents who use sex services purchase sex

- more than 500 times 2%
- once 7%
- 101 – 500 times 14%
- 2 – 5 times 21%
- 51 – 100 times 11%
- 6 – 10 times 11%
- 11 – 50 times 34%

THE PICK-UP

Internet survey of where men who use sex services meet their sex sellers

- on the street 56%
- escort services 57%
- massage parlors 59%
- clubs or bars 36%
- hotels 26%
- brothels 45%
- through advertisements 45%

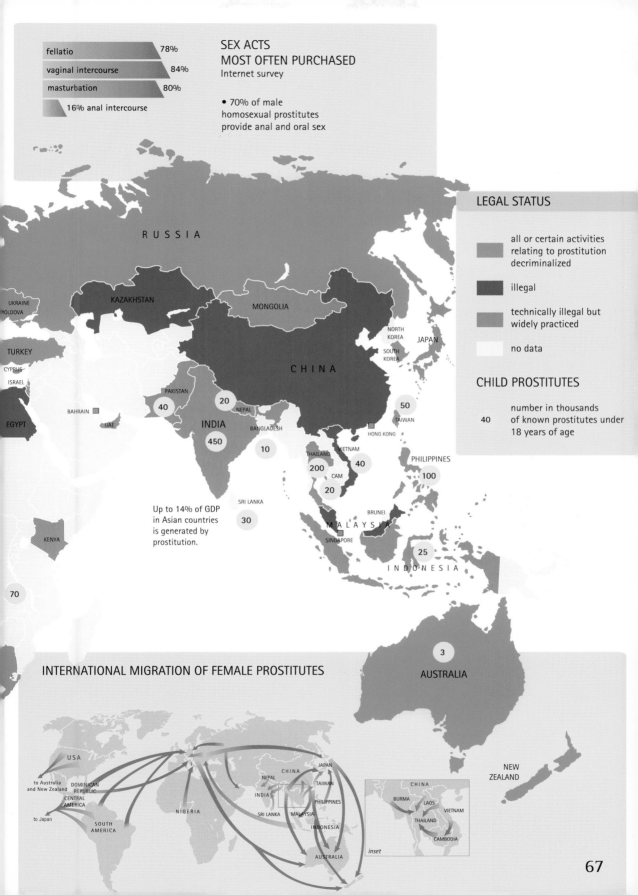

RUSSIA

KAZAKHSTAN

MONGOLIA

UKRAINE
MOLDOVA

NORTH
KOREA

SOUTH
KOREA

JAPAN

TURKEY

CYPRUS

ISRAEL

CHINA

EGYPT

PAKISTAN

40

20

NEPAL

50

BAHRAIN

TAIWAN

UAE

INDIA

BANGLADESH

450

HONG KONG

10

VIETNAM

THAILAND

40

PHILIPPINES

200

CAM

100

SRI LANKA

20

Up to 14% of GDP in Asian countries is generated by prostitution.

30

BRUNEI

KENYA

MALAYSIA

SINGAPORE

25

INDONESIA

70

3

AUSTRALIA

NEW
ZEALAND

LEGAL STATUS

■ all or certain activities relating to prostitution decriminalized

■ illegal

■ technically illegal but widely practiced

□ no data

CHILD PROSTITUTES

40 number in thousands of known prostitutes under 18 years of age

INTERNATIONAL MIGRATION OF FEMALE PROSTITUTES

USA

to Australia
and New Zealand

DOMINICAN
REPUBLIC

CENTRAL
AMERICA

to Japan

SOUTH
AMERICA

NIGERIA

NEPAL

CHINA

INDIA

SRI LANKA

JAPAN

TAIWAN

PHILIPPINES

MALAYSIA

INDONESIA

AUSTRALIA

CHINA

BURMA

LAOS

VIETNAM

THAILAND

CAMBODIA

inset

SEX TOURISM

Thriving sex tourism industries have developed in many of the world's popular holiday destinations, boosting the income of poorer nations. People whose livelihoods are linked to tourism, including bar and brothel owners, taxi and rickshaw drivers, guides and even parents, readily offer children to tourists for sex.

MALE HOMOSEXUAL SEX TOURISTS

USA
to Asia

WESTERN EUROPE

KENYA

SENEGAL
GAMBIA

from USA

EUROPE

NEPAL

INDIA
Goa

SRI LANKA

INDONESIA
Bali

AUSTRALIA   NEW ZEALAND

USA

CARIBBEAN

ARRESTS IN ASIA
Countries' shares of tourists arrested for sexual abuse of children in Asia

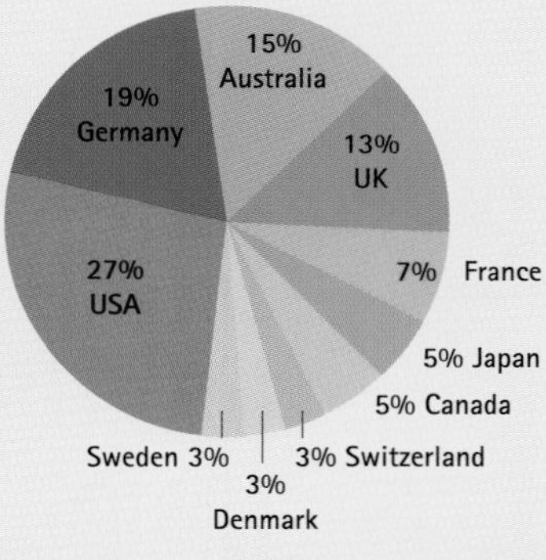

- 15% Australia
- 19% Germany
- 13% UK
- 27% USA
- 7% France
- 5% Japan
- 5% Canada
- 3% Switzerland
- Sweden 3%
- 3% Denmark

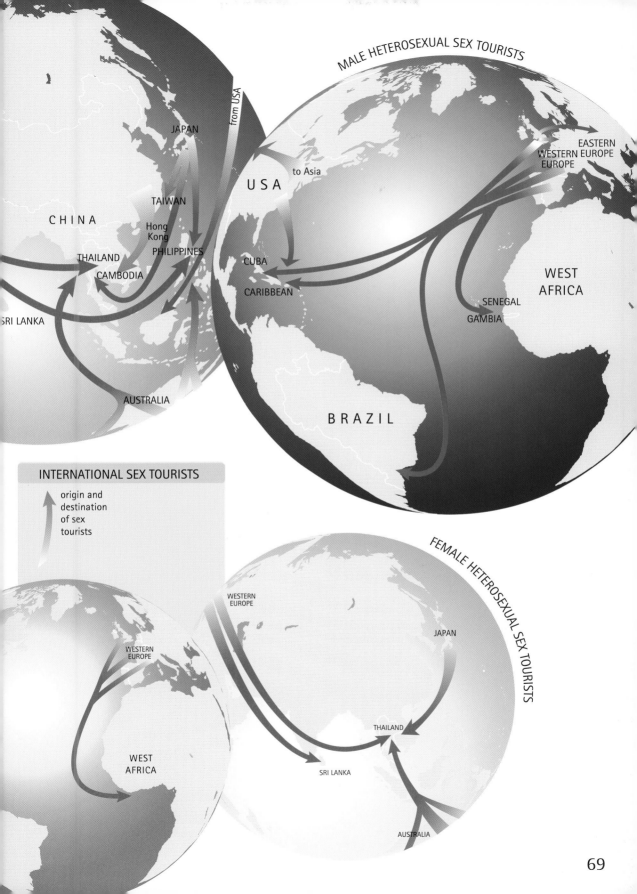

MALE HETEROSEXUAL SEX TOURISTS

from USA

JAPAN

to Asia

USA

TAIWAN

CHINA

Hong Kong

PHILIPPINES

THAILAND

CUBA

CAMBODIA

CARIBBEAN

SRI LANKA

EASTERN WESTERN EUROPE
EUROPE

WEST AFRICA

SENEGAL

GAMBIA

AUSTRALIA

BRAZIL

INTERNATIONAL SEX TOURISTS

origin and destination of sex tourists

WESTERN EUROPE

WESTERN EUROPE

WEST AFRICA

FEMALE HETEROSEXUAL SEX TOURISTS

WESTERN EUROPE

JAPAN

THAILAND

SRI LANKA

AUSTRALIA

Part Six SEXUAL RITES

"No woman can call herself free who doesn't own
and control her own body."

— Marie Stopes (1880-1958)

RELIGION

Religion pronounces on most sexual issues – such as pre-marital sex and extra-marital sex, adultery, masturbation, celibacy, homosexuality, and abortion. There has been variance between core religious doctrines and their interpretation at different times throughout history. There are dissimilarities in practices between different countries or societies, different sects of the same religion, between young and old followers, and between conservatives and liberals. In addition, adherents may not follow official religious teaching — for example, the Catholic church condemns birth control, but many Catholics use contraception.

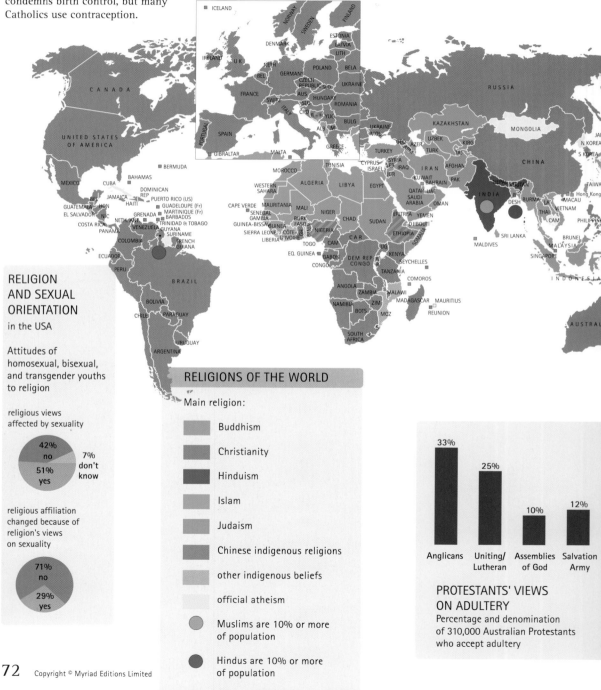

RELIGION AND SEXUAL ORIENTATION
in the USA

Attitudes of homosexual, bisexual, and transgender youths to religion

religious views affected by sexuality

- 42% no
- 7% don't know
- 51% yes

religious affiliation changed because of religion's views on sexuality

- 71% no
- 29% yes

RELIGIONS OF THE WORLD

Main religion:

- Buddhism
- Christianity
- Hinduism
- Islam
- Judaism
- Chinese indigenous religions
- other indigenous beliefs
- official atheism
- Muslims are 10% or more of population
- Hindus are 10% or more of population

PROTESTANTS' VIEWS ON ADULTERY

Percentage and denomination of 310,000 Australian Protestants who accept adultery

- Anglicans 33%
- Uniting/ Lutheran 25%
- Assemblies of God 10%
- Salvation Army 12%

BUDDHISM

prohibits

- Marriage for monks.
- Women touching monks.
- Women entering temples when menstruating.

Four Noble Truths:

All life is suffering;

Suffering derives from desire;

Suffering will cease when desire is quelled;

Desire can be quelled through morality, meditation and wisdom.

CHRISTIANITY

prohibits

- Extra-marital sex.
- Lusting after another's spouse.
- Marriage for Catholic priests and nuns.
- Divorce for Catholics.

HINDUSIM

Baghavad Gita **encourages** celibacy and meditation for men over 50 to promote health and longevity.

The Kama Sutra **encourages** understanding of sex and explains sexual practices.

The wedding ceremony is the most important Hindu sacrament.

ISLAM

prohibits

- Sex during menstruation and Ramadan.
- Menstruating women to perform prayers or to touch or read the *Koran*.
- Masturbation.
- Homosexuality.
- Anal sex.
- Mixing with opposite sex after puberty.
- Male lust for women.
- Equal divorce rights for women.

allows

- Polygamy (up to four wives).

JUDAISM

prohibits

- Extra-marital sex.

expects

- Male circumcision.

MARIANA ISLANDS

KIRIBATI

BOUGAINVILLE

PAPUA NEW GUINEA

SOLOMON ISLANDS

WESTERN SAMOA

FIJI

TONGA

NEW CALEDONIA

NEW ZEALAND

OFFICIAL POSITIONS

- condemned or unacceptable
- no clear position
- acceptable in most cases
- accepted

religion · masturbation · pre-marital sex · extra-marital sex · homosexual sex

BUDDHISM

CHRISTIANITY — Baptists, Methodists

HINDUISM

ISLAM

JUDAISM

FEMALE GENITAL EXCISION

Female genital excision (FGE) is a surgical procedure carried out daily on 6,000 girls between 4 and 10 years of age. It is usually performed by female relatives with crude instruments and without anaesthetic. Many communities regard it as an essential prerequisite for a girl to become a woman, marriageable, and faithful.

FGE can vary in scope from the removal of a small part of the clitoris to major excision of the entire labia and clitoris, after which the wound is sewn up leaving a small orifice, sewn up again after childbirth, on divorce and on her husband's death. FGE can lead to immediate infection, bleeding, pain, and death; long-term problems include pain on sexual intercourse and dangers in childbirth.

UK:
10,000 girls risk undergoing FGE, mainly those from Eritrea, Ethiopia, Somalia, and Yemen.

France:
32,500 women have had FGE. Most are from Mali, and a few from Senegal.

CANADA

USA

USA:
168,000 women have had FGE.

LIBYA

MAURITANIA

MALI

NIGER

CHAD

SENEGAL
GAMBIA
GUINEA
BISSAU GUINEA
SIERRA
LEONE LIBERIA

CÔTE
D'IVOIRE
GHANA
TOGO
BENIN
BURKINA
FASO

NIGERIA

NORWAY
SWEDEN
FINLAND
DENMARK
UK
GERMANY
BELGIUM
FRANCE
ITALY

CAMEROON

CAR

DEM REP
CONGO

CONGO

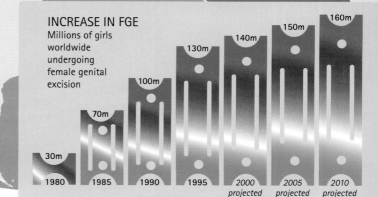

INCREASE IN FGE
Millions of girls worldwide undergoing female genital excision

1980	1985	1990	1995	2000 projected	2005 projected	2010 projected
30m	70m	100m	130m	140m	150m	160m

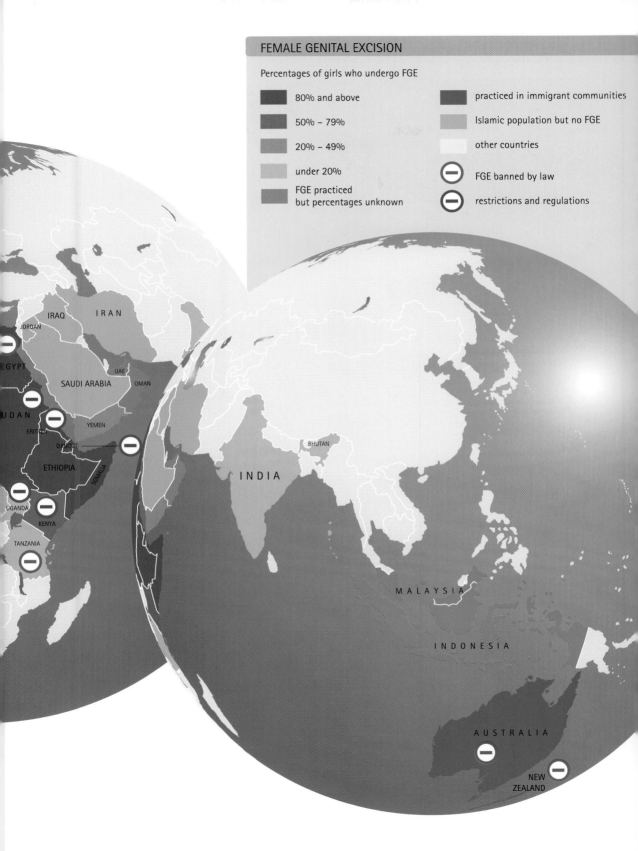

FEMALE GENITAL EXCISION

Percentages of girls who undergo FGE

- 80% and above
- 50% – 79%
- 20% – 49%
- under 20%
- FGE practiced but percentages unknown
- practiced in immigrant communities
- Islamic population but no FGE
- other countries
- FGE banned by law
- restrictions and regulations

JORDAN
IRAQ
IRAN
EGYPT
SAUDI ARABIA
UAE
OMAN
SUDAN
YEMEN
ERITREA
DJIBOUTI
ETHIOPIA
SOMALIA
UGANDA
KENYA
TANZANIA

BHUTAN
INDIA
MALAYSIA
INDONESIA
AUSTRALIA
NEW ZEALAND

CIRCUMCISION

Worldwide, 23 percent of men are circumcised.
Each year 13 million circumcisions
are carried out.

C A N A D A

UNITED STATES
OF AMERICA

MOROCCO TUNISIA

WESTERN
SAHARA ALGERIA

MAURITANIA

SENEGAL
GAMBIA MALI
GUINEA NIGER

TURKEY

SYRIA

ISRAEL JOR.

LIBYA EGYPT

SUDAN

DJIBOUTI

UK

TRENDS IN CIRCUMCISION
in the USA

Percentage of males
circumcised

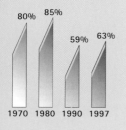

80% 85%
           59% 63%

1970 1980 1990 1997

CIRCUMCISED MEN

Percentages of circumcised men
where known

- over 50%
- 25%
- under 10%
- no data

In a US poll of 313 men contacting circumcision information groups, 60% complained of a lack of natural wholeness, 50% of feelings of parental violation, and 11% of painful erections.

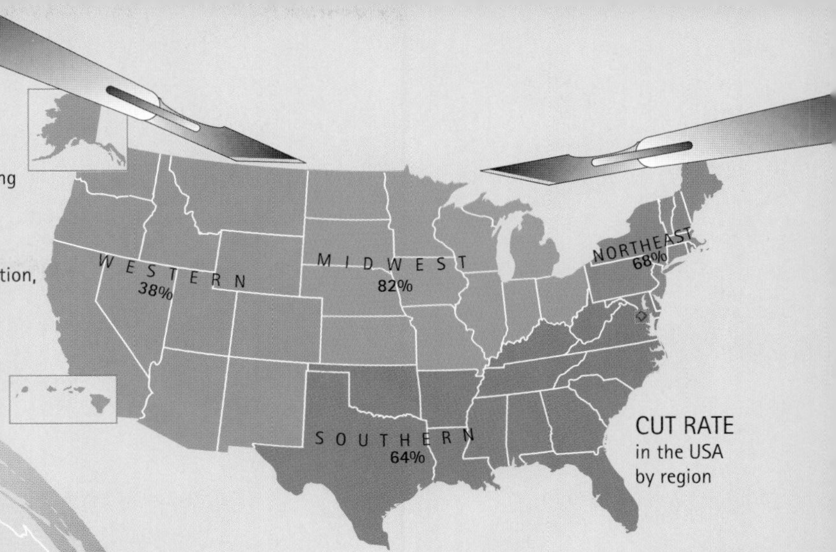

W E S T E R N
38%

M I D W E S T
82%

NORTHEAST
68%

S O U T H E R N
64%

CUT RATE
in the USA
by region

In the USA, 63% of men are circumcised each year: 1.2 million men or one every 26 seconds.

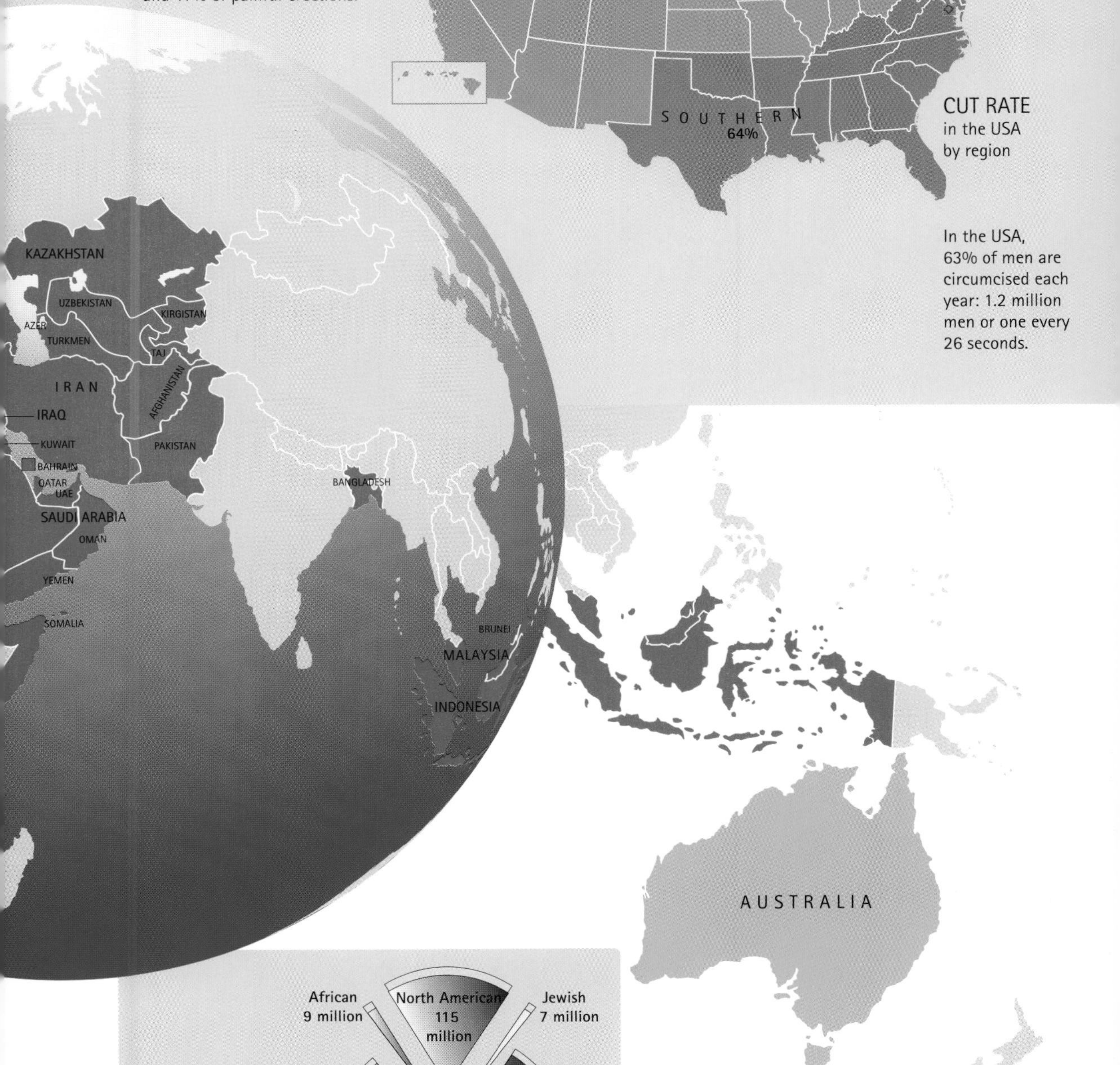

KAZAKHSTAN

UZBEKISTAN

AZER
TURKMEN

KIRGISTAN

TAJ

AFGHANISTAN

I R A N

IRAQ

KUWAIT

PAKISTAN

BAHRAIN
QATAR
UAE

BANGLADESH

SAUDI ARABIA

OMAN

YEMEN

SOMALIA

BRUNEI

MALAYSIA

INDONESIA

AUSTRALIA

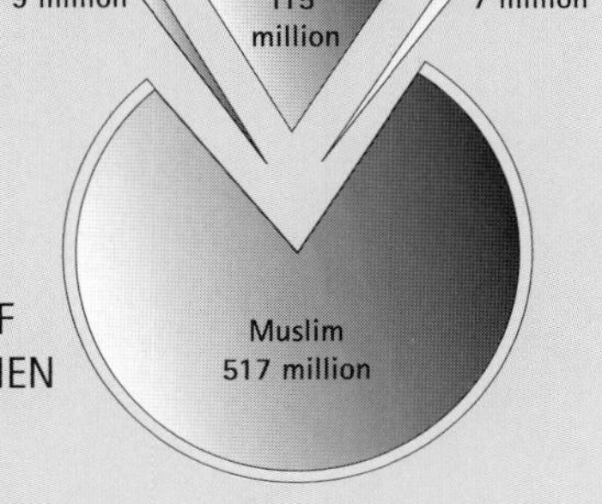

African
9 million

North American
115 million

Jewish
7 million

Muslim
517 million

DISTRIBUTION OF CIRCUMCISED MEN WORLDWIDE

"Those who lift and drop a rock will not only hurt the feet of others, but also their own."

— Chinese proverb

SEXUAL HARASSMENT AND STALKING

Sexual harassment includes leering, lewd gestures, touching, grabbing or deliberately brushing up against another person, requests for sexual favors, derogatory remarks, questions about a person's sex life, obscene jokes, offensive pictures or photographs. It also includes stalking, which is frequently the result of someone refusing to accept the breakdown of a sexual or emotional relationship.

Sexual harassment can take place in any context, and especially at work where it may include the additional threat of job loss.

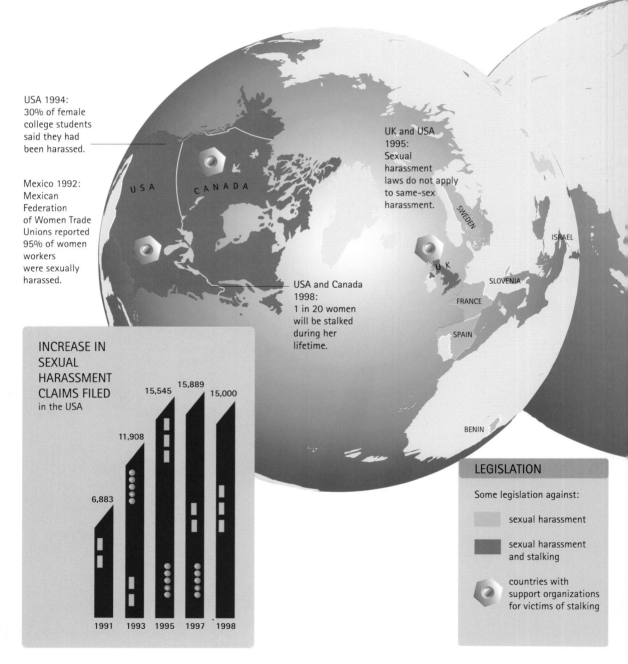

USA 1994:
30% of female college students said they had been harassed.

Mexico 1992: Mexican Federation of Women Trade Unions reported 95% of women workers were sexually harassed.

UK and USA 1995: Sexual harassment laws do not apply to same-sex harassment.

USA and Canada 1998: 1 in 20 women will be stalked during her lifetime.

SWEDEN
ISRAEL
SLOVENIA
FRANCE
SPAIN
BENIN
USA
CANADA
U K

INCREASE IN SEXUAL HARASSMENT CLAIMS FILED
in the USA

- 6,883 — 1991
- 11,908 — 1993
- 15,545 — 1995
- 15,889 — 1997
- 15,000 — 1998

LEGISLATION

Some legislation against:

- sexual harassment
- sexual harassment and stalking
- countries with support organizations for victims of stalking

CYBER-HARASSMENT
in 1999

50% of employees with internet access at work receive adult-oriented, racist, sexist or improper email.

Over one million women reported online harassment.

20% of employers received complaints about the appropriateness of email.

85% of US employers have policies to avert harassing emails.

Japan 1998: 40% of working women reported sexual harassment

JAPAN

TAIWAN

Hong Kong

Taiwan 1999: 27% of medical students reported being sexually harassed.

Australia 1996: 30% of 14,000 women naval personnel and civilian employees reported harassment.

AUSTRALIA

NEW ZEALAND

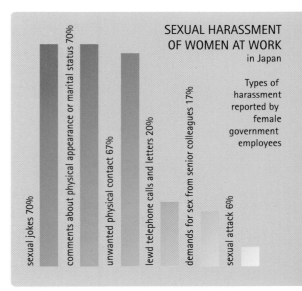

SEXUAL HARASSMENT OF WOMEN AT WORK
in Japan

Types of harassment reported by female government employees

- sexual jokes 70%
- comments about physical appearance or marital status 70%
- unwanted physical contact 67%
- lewd telephone calls and letters 20%
- demands for sex from senior colleagues 17%
- sexual attack 6%

HOMOPHOBIC HARASSMENT AT SCHOOL
in the USA

Anti-homosexual behavior or violence in high schools reported by homosexual, bisexual, and transgender young men and women

• 68% of US high schools have policies to protect students and staff from homophobic harassment.

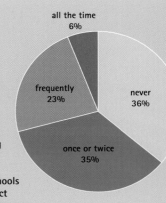

- all the time 6%
- frequently 23%
- never 36%
- once or twice 35%

SEXUAL HARASSMENT OF WOMEN AT WORK
in the UK

harasser senior to victim 74%

harasser loses job 5%

victim either dismissed or resigns from job 77%

81

SEXUAL VIOLENCE

Sexual violence includes rape, sexual assault, sexual harassment, and child sexual abuse such as incest and pedophilia. Many offences are unreported because of shame and fear of reprisals. In most cases, the assailant is known to the victim.

UK:
3% of men report adult male rape. Over 5% of men report that they were sexually abused as children.

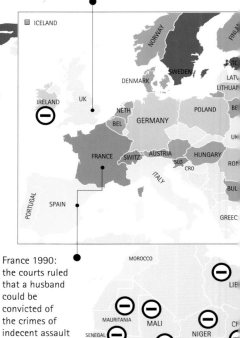

Canada, and other countries that are most successful at prosecuting sex abusers, appear to have the highest incidence of offenders, while those countries where sexual abuse is largely ignored by society, appear to have a low incidence.

USA:
50% of reported rapes occur in the victim's home.

France 1990:
the courts ruled that a husband could be convicted of the crimes of indecent assault and of raping his wife.

Spain 1999:
Of 213 rape victims, 20% contracted an STI and 10% became pregnant.

REOFFENDERS
in Canada

Reconviction rate of 86 rapists reoffending within five years of end of prison term

- 27% re-offending any criminal act
- 13% re-offending violent crimes
- 8% re-offending sexual crimes
- 52% non-offending

FEMALE RAPE

Reported rapes per 10,000 women

- over 4
- 2 – 4
- 1.3 – 1.9
- 1 – 1.2
- under 1
- no data
- ⊖ abortion only permitted to save life of woman

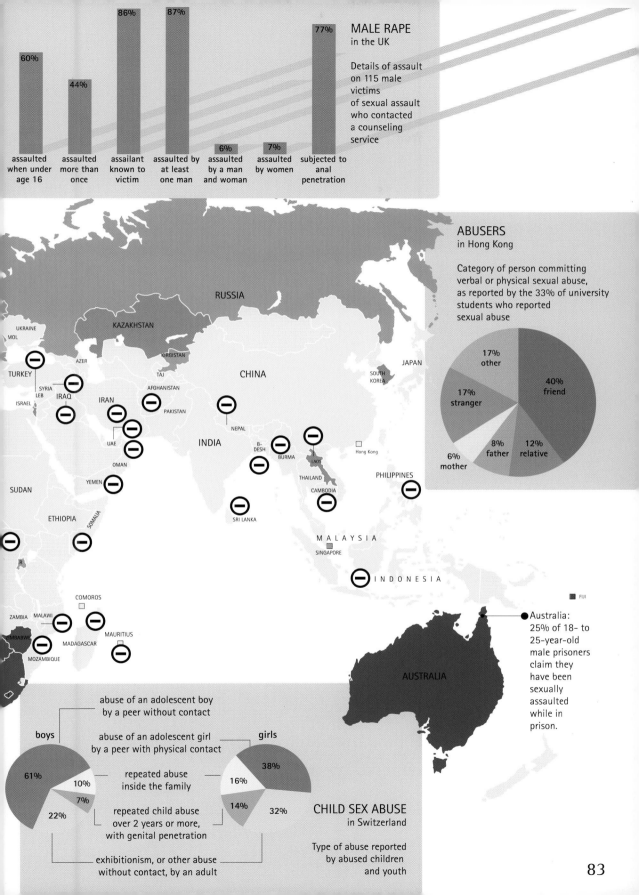

MALE RAPE
in the UK

Details of assault on 115 male victims of sexual assault who contacted a counseling service

- 60% assaulted when under age 16
- 44% assaulted more than once
- 86% assailant known to victim
- 87% assaulted by at least one man
- 6% assaulted by a man and woman
- 7% assaulted by women
- 77% subjected to anal penetration

ABUSERS
in Hong Kong

Category of person committing verbal or physical sexual abuse, as reported by the 33% of university students who reported sexual abuse

- 40% friend
- 17% other
- 17% stranger
- 6% mother
- 8% father
- 12% relative

Australia: 25% of 18- to 25-year-old male prisoners claim they have been sexually assaulted while in prison.

CHILD SEX ABUSE
in Switzerland

Type of abuse reported by abused children and youth

boys
- 61%
- 10%
- 7%
- 22%

girls
- 38%
- 16%
- 14%
- 32%

- abuse of an adolescent boy by a peer without contact
- abuse of an adolescent girl by a peer with physical contact
- repeated abuse inside the family
- repeated child abuse over 2 years or more, with genital penetration
- exhibitionism, or other abuse without contact, by an adult

Map labels: UKRAINE, MOL, RUSSIA, KAZAKHSTAN, KIRGISTAN, AZER, TAJ, TURKEY, SYRIA, LEB, ISRAEL, IRAQ, IRAN, AFGHANISTAN, PAKISTAN, CHINA, SOUTH KOREA, JAPAN, UAE, OMAN, NEPAL, INDIA, B-DESH, BURMA, LAOS, THAILAND, CAMBODIA, Hong Kong, PHILIPPINES, SUDAN, YEMEN, ETHIOPIA, SOMALIA, SRI LANKA, MALAYSIA, SINGAPORE, INDONESIA, COMOROS, ZAMBIA, MALAWI, MADAGASCAR, MAURITIUS, ZIMBABWE, MOZAMBIQUE, AUSTRALIA, FIJI

83

84

Part Eight EVOLUTIONS

"Of the basic human drives for food, shelter and sex,
sex is probably the biggest driver of
new services and technologies."

— Ian Pearson,
futurologist, 1998

THE FUTURE OF SEX

LAW

HEALTH AND
REPRODUCTION

Sex is increasingly
separated from
reproduction.
Laws, religion,
health and social
systems will
struggle to keep
up with new
technological
developments
which enable
varied, creative
and diverse sexual
activities to
flourish.

2000–2010

Abolition of death penalty for adultery
and homosexuality.

Contraception legally available in all
countries.

Human cloning makes asexual
reproduction possible.

2010–2020

Sex laws subject to international
review.

50% of rape cases taken to court.

Tighter transborder controls to deter
sex tourism and pedophilia.

Designer babies increasingly
common.

New forms of birth control
invented.

New treatment for spinal cord
injuries enables sexual
intercourse.

2020–2030

Homosexuality decriminalized
worldwide.

Cloning for infertile couples legalized.

Cloning a practical alternative
for infertile couples.

New viral STI kills millions
worldwide.

2030–2040

Abortion decriminalized worldwide.

Ban on all religions, organizations,
institutions, and social clubs that
discriminate on the basis of sexual
orientation.

Pharmaceuticals developed to treat
worldwide STI epidemic.

Transplants of ovaries and testes.

Genetic manipulation of gender.

2025 SEX CITIES
Centers of sex parties, real-time and
virtual-reality sex, commercial sexual
entertainment, sex information and
advice, counseling, sales booths
for sex toys and sex aids.

● city

2040–2050

All sex acts between consenting adults
in private decriminalized.

Puberty occurs one year earlier
than in 2000.

Vancouver
San Francisco
Denver
New York
Atlanta
Cancun
Caracas
Edinburgh
London
Madrid
Ibiza
Moscow
Amsterdam
Istanbul
Wuhan
Shanghai
Bangalore
Manila
Bangkok
Jakarta
Rio de Janeiro
Sydney

SEXUAL PRACTICES	SEXUAL ORIENTATION	RELIGION	CYBERSEX
Health benefits of sexual abstinence, cybersex, and monophilia promoted. Sex on the moon is proved to last longer as bodies move more slowly.	First Global Gay Pride Festival is coordinated via internet in 50 cities. Same-sex couples in industrialized countries allowed to adopt children.	The Roman Catholic Church allows non-abortion methods of contraception. Same-sex unions accepted.	Cybersex is a massive growth industry. In response, the physical body is increasingly tattoed, pierced, reconstructed, and genetically retrained.
Conservative backlash attacks adventurous sexual activities. Orgasm chip implanted in brain.	Human Genome Project discovers whether there is a genetic basis for homosexuality.	All religions recognise that: • a continuum of sexual orientation exists, established in youth and essentially unchangeable; • since sexual orientation is not a matter of choice, it cannot be sinful.	One third of couples in rich countries meet their partners through cyberdating. Most sex education and counseling is online. Cyber-blackmail develops as terrorists hack into personal sex files.
Genetic modification and cloning enables growth of additional sex organs, designed for pleasure.	People increasingly anamorphic, androgenous, ambisextrous and polyamorous, both in real or virtual time.	All religions accept that masturbation is not a sin. New religious movement develops, based on humanity and equality of sexual persuasions. Persons of all sexual orientations accepted as clergy.	Virtual-reality sex becomes possible, accompanied by hologram of choice. Marriage rates decline as cybersex increases. Cybersex becomes grounds for divorce.
Artificial penis invented. Sexual-experience chips downloaded directly to the brain from internet.	People become unfaithful to their original gender and many have floating identities.	Sexual orientation will become a non-issue in most religions.	Computer virus wipes out cybersex.
Most sex for pleasure rather than procreation. Global population reaches nine billion.	Boundaries of physical, sexual, and emotional identities constantly stretched and changed.	Discrimination against minority sexual orientations, like racism and sexism in earlier years, will be condemned as institutional hatred.	World Institute of Human Sexual Relationships founded to teach relationships and personal intimacy.

BC C5 Female buttocks feature on figurines.

BC C4 China: fashion for small-waisted women.

BC C3 Homosexuality, transsexualism, transvestitism, and masturbation reported as common sexual practices.

BC C3 India and Egypt: elephant and crocodile dung used as vaginal barrier contraceptive.

BC C3 West Africa: male circumcision practiced.

BC 1550 Egypt: Acacia tips, dates and honey used as contraceptive.

BC C2 China: Emperor Shih Huang Ti, chronicled sexual practices, conception, infertility, impotence, and sex techniques for curing backache, hemorrhoids, deafness, and indigestion. Ejaculation believed to cause weakness, even the loss of men's Taoist souls.

BC C1 Middle East: circumcision practiced.

AD C1 Nile Valley and Arabia: Female Genital Excision practiced.

AD C3 India: Vatsyayana writes *Kama Sutra*, linking sexual pleasure to physical and spiritual well-being.

1000 Christian Church first involved with marriages.

1500 UK: Average age of puberty was 19 years.

1791 France: Ban on homosexuality repealed.

1825–1895 Germany: Karl Heinrich Ulrichs campaigned for homosexual rights.

1886 Germany: Richard Freiherr von Krafft-Ebing (1840-1902), author of *Pyschopathia Sexualis*, claimed masturbation led to insanity and homosexuality was a disease.

1860s Austria: Gregor Johann Mendel described genetic inheritance.

1883 UK: Richard Burton (1821-1890) translated *Kama Sutra*.

1890 UK: Average age of puberty was 15 years.

1895 Austria: Sigmund Freud (1856-1939), founder of psychoanalysis, claimed in *Studies in Hysteria* that neurosis resulted from early sexual relations between children and adults.

1899 UK: first prosecution of an "immoral" film.

early 1900s Russia: Ivan Petrovich Pavlov (1849-1936) advocated reconditioning of sexual tastes through aversion therapy.

1900s UK: FGE used as a cure for epilepsy, hysteria, nymphomania, masturbation.

1900s Europe and North America: male circumcision recommended to stop masturbation.

1897–1910 UK: Henry Havelock Ellis (1859-1939), author of *Sexual Inversion* and *Studies in the Psychology of Sex* (10 vols.), proposed that homosexuality was not a disease and women might enjoy sex, and advocated sex education.

1913 UK: British Board of Film Censorship first banned nudity.

1918 UK: Marie Stopes (1880-1958), caused a furore by campaigning for sexual and reproductive rights for women. Her books, *Married Love* and *Wise Parenthood*, were worldwide bestsellers despite being strongly condemned by the church, and by the political and medical establishments.

1921 UK's first birth control clinic opened by Marie Stopes.

1925 USA: Margaret Sanger (1880-1966), author of *The Woman Rebel* and *Family Limitation* and campaigner for women's rights to contraception and sexual pleasure, opened first American birth control clinic.

1925 First international birth control conference.

1925 Germany: Magnus Hirschfield (1868-1935) published *Homosexuality of Man and Women* and, in 1938, *Sexual anomalies and Perversions*. Founded first institute of Sexology in Berlin. Campaigned for homosexual and lesbians rights.

1927 Austria and UK: Wilhelm Reich (1897-1957) published *The Function of the Orgasm* and emphasized orgasm as the goal of therapy.

1928 UK: Penicillin discovered by Alexander Fleming.

1945–46 Sweden: Elise Ottesen-Jensen organized International Planned Parenthood Federation (IPPF).

1947 USA: Alfred C. Kinsey (1894-1956) founded the Institute for Sex Research (now The Kinsey Institute) at the University of Indiana.

1947 Japan: Shin'ichi Asayama surveyed sexual behavior of Japanese students and followed up for over 30 years.

1947 UK and USA: penicillin used to cure sexually-transmitted infections.

1948 India: *The International Journal of Sexology* first published.

1950 USA: Gynecologist Ernst Gräfenberg described female ejaculation and the G-spot.

1951 Denmark: First transgender surgery, male to female.

1951 USA: Homosexual liberation organization, the "Mattachine Society" founded.

1953 USA: The Kinsey Report on 12,000 people described premarital and extramarital intercourse, women's sexual capacities, and the extent of homosexual behavior, and was attacked by conservative religious and political leaders.

1953 Germany and USA: Harry Benjamin introduced the term "transsexuals", to distinguish them from transvestites.

1959 Democratic Republic of Congo: First HIV later detected in blood specimen of adult Bantu man.

1960 Modern birth control: "the Pill".

1964 USA: Sexuality and Information Council of the USA (SIECUS) founded.

1965 USA: The Kinsey Institute published *Sex Offenders: An Analysis of Types.*

1966 USA: William H. Masters and Virginia Johnson published *Human Sexual Response,* reporting the importance of clitoris, and showing women could have multiple orgasms.

1970 USA: Masters and Johnson published *Human Sexual Inadequacy,* which becomes the basis for a new behavioral sex therapy.

1971 Australia: Derek Llewellyn-Jones, published *Everywomen* and, in 1981, *Everyman.*

1973 Australia: first "gay marriage".

1973 USA: American Psychiatric Association stated homosexuality is not an illness.

1973 USA: Nancy Friday published *My Secret Garden: Women's Sexual Fantasies.*

1974 UK: Alex Comfort published sex manual, *The Joy of Sex.*

1974 World Health Organization (WHO) convened a meeting of sexologists and publishes the report *Education and Treatment in Human Sexuality: The Training of Health Professionals.*

1974 France: First World Congress of Sexology held in Paris.

1974 UK: forerunner of British Association for Sexual and Marital Therapy (BASMT) formed.

1976 USA: Shere Hite published *The Hite Report: A Nationwide Study of Female Sexuality* and, in 1978, *The Hite Report on Male Sexuality,* reporting sexual preferences and practices of thousands of men and women.

1976 France: Michel Foucault (1926-84), philosopher and historian, de-medicalized sex with the publication of *The History of Sexuality.*

1977 UK: Charlotte Wolff published *Bisexuality: A Study.*

1978 UK: First test-tube baby.

1978 UK: Emily L. Sisley & Bertha Harris published *The Joy of Lesbian Sex.*

1979 UK: Desmond Morris, author of *The Naked Ape* (1967), published *Intimate Behavior,* showing human behavior is not very different from that of many animals.

1978 World Association for Sexology founded.

1981 USA: first cases of HIV / AIDS.

1982 France: First court case on FGE, after a baby died.

1986 WHO and IPPF condemn FGE.

1990 USA: California became the first state to criminalize stalking.

1990s Surrogate mothers.

1990s USA: "Dr Ruth" Westheimer brought sex into the TV talk show.

1990 France: Court ruled that a husband can be convicted for indecently assaulting and raping his wife.

1991 India: First International Conference on Orgasm.

1992 China: publication of *Sexual Behavior in Modern China: Report of the Nationwide Survey of 20,000 Men and Women.*

1993 China: First sex shop opened, in Beijing.

1994 USA: National survey of 3,500 Americans surprised many by reporting most Americans are monogamous.

1994 UK: Largest national survey of sexual behavior, *National Survey of Sexual Attitudes and Lifestyles,* published.

1994 Germany: Robert Koch Institute in Berlin opened Archive for Sexology.

1995 UK: Church of England denied gay man right to be godfather to his sister's son.

1995 UK: First private prosecution for rape brought by two prostitutes after police refused to act. Defendant jailed for 14 years.

1996 UK: Man jailed for downloading pornography from internet.

1996 Germany: 1.5 million Catholics signed petition opposing Pope's views on celibate priesthood and sexual morality.

1996 Brazil: Catholic Bishop refused to marry paraplegic man, because he was incapable of having sex and fathering children.

1997 India: First National Convention of Sex Workers.

1997 USA: Child sex offenders named on the internet.

1997 Spain: World Congress of Sexology issued declaration of sexual rights.

1998: UK: Average age of puberty was 13 years.

1998 Korea: Human embryo cloned.

1998 Germany: ISP convicted for failing to block child pornography on internet site.

1998 Israel: Defense Forces first described sexual harassment as a crime.

1998 Viagra launched for treatment of impotence.

2001 France: 15th World Congress of Sexology, in Paris.

APHRODISIACS

Aphrodisiacs are any drugs, food, drinks, plant, animal parts, smells, or objects which are believed to increase sexual desire. They are distinct from mixtures and medicines used to treat impotence.

Aphrodisiacs are mainly bought and used by men, either on themselves or on, often unsuspecting, women. Romance is said to be the aphrodisiac for women.

Aphrodisiacs are named after Aphrodite, the Greek Goddess of love, fertility, eroticism, childbearing, and bountiful crops. The early Greeks, Arabs, Egyptians, and Hindus strongly believed in aphrodisiacs. In the 20th century, pornography and romantic novels replaced many of the traditional aphrodisiacs.

ALCOHOL
Small amounts relax inhibitions; larger quantities diminish male performance.

ALMONDS

ARTICHOKES
Catherine de Medici's favorite.

ASPARAGUS
Most prized of all the erotic vegetables in many cultures due to its phallic appearance. Madame de Pompadour, the mistress of Louis XV of France, ate little but asparagus and egg yolks. Asparagus has been an ingredient of love potions through the ages, reported in Hindu love treatises and used in modern Indian recipes for strengthening lost vigor.

BASIL
An aromatic plant, said to help the deficiency of Venus, used by Italian girls.

BIRD'S NEST SOUP
A popular soup from China, composed of sea-swallow nests and edible seaweed. The leaves are stuck together by fish spawn.

BRAIN
The most important sex organ.

BROAD BEAN SOUP
From Italy.

CARAWAY

CARDAMOM

CARROTS
Arabs' favorite, especially cooked in milk.

CELERY

CHEESE
Popular in 18th-century France. Parmesan was a special favorite. Gorgonzola was also used as an aphrodisiac.

CHESTNUTS

CHICKPEAS

CHOCOLATE
Scientifically proven to be psycho-sensual.

CORIANDER
Important to Greeks, Romans Egyptians, Hindus, and Chinese. Ingredient of many ancient love potions.

DILL

DRUGS
Marijuana, amyl nitrates, cocaine, ecstasy, all relax inhibitions but also may endanger life. In 1995 four men in the USA died after ingesting digoxin, a heart stimulant made from foxgloves.

EGGS
Used worldwide through the ages. Egg yolk mixed with saffron is a favorite Muslim aphrodisiac.

ENDIVE

ERYNGO
Maidens anxious to preserve their chastity in the Middle Ages were warned off eryngo or sea holly, a root that can grow two meters in length.

FENNEL
Used by Egyptians, Greeks, Romans, Hindus.

FRUIT
Most fruits have been considered aphrodisiacs, especially bananas, figs, peaches, pineapples, cherries, grapes, mangos.

FUGU
The liver of the deadly fugu, or pufferfish, is eaten by Japanese to make them more virile — if they survive.

GAME
Venison, goose and guinea fowl. Also pheasant and pigeon meat, due to the elaborate courtship ritual of the birds.

GARLIC
European and Oriental erotologists include garlic as an aphrodisiac ingredient. Among the Ainu of Japan, garlic was as nectar and ambrosia to Greek gods.

GINGER

GINSENG

HALIBUT

HARICOT BEANS

HENNA
Arabs believe it to be an aphrodisiac when rubbed on fingers, skull, and feet.

HERRING ROES

HONEY

INSECTS
Spanish fly is the best-known aphrodisiac, made by grinding the bright green Cantharis beetle into a fine, dried powder which irritates the bladder and urethra; the resultant tingling and burning is said to be sexually exciting, although it can cause blistering and even death. Spanish fly may be ingested or rubbed on the genitals. The Marquis de Sade laced sweets with Spanish fly, leading to the admonition by parents that persists to this day: "Never take sweets from a stranger."

JASMINE
Fragrance, favored by Cleopatra and reported in Indian love texts.

KITCHEN SMELLS
Smell of baking cinnamon rolls is said to increase penile blood flow, resulting in erections; oranges; pumpkin pie with lavender; donut; or donut with black licorice.

LAUREL LEAVES

LAVENDER

LENTILS

LIVER
Shark liver in China and Japan.

MANDRAKE ROOT
Mentioned in the Bible as a fertility drug.

MEAT
Swan meat has been favored as an aphrodisiac because of lifelong fidelity, yet others prefer rabbit meat because of the reverse. In Africa, hippopotamus meat is a favorite.

MUSHROOMS
Used by Egyptians, Greeks, Romans.

NAIL PARINGS
Used by the Romans.

NUTMEG

ONIONS

OYSTERS

PARSLEY
Used by Greeks and Romans.

PHEROMES
Perfumes now contain pheromes, known to attract sexually.

POWER
Powerful people can always attract desirable partners.

PRECIOUS STONES
Pastilles of powdered ambergris, rubies, gold and pearls were once popular in Persia.

QUEEN BEE
Royal jelly is a valued aphrodisiac, especially in China.

ROCKET
The plant rocket was sown around the base of statues of Priapus to restore vigor to the genitalia. In medieval times, the Church frowned on the lechery associated with the plant, and banned its cultivation in monastic gardens.

SEALS
Seals are only one of two animals with a bone in their penis and are a favorite Asian aphrodisiac.

SPINACH

TESTICLES AND OTHER GENITALIA
Early sex manuals included recipes for preparing the genitalia of dogs, bulls, deer, and alligator. Goat testicles, boiled in milk, are popular in India.

THYME
Frequently mentioned as an aphrodisiac.

TOMATOES

TRUFFLES

UNDERPANTS
A Japanese company impregnates male underpants with a tiny pherome capsule, which breaks on friction, wafting a seductive perfume into the air.

VALENTINE'S DAY
St Valentine was put to death on February 14, AD270 after disobeying the instructions of Claudius II and continuing secretly to marry couples in love. The Roman ruler believed marriage made soldiers weak and ineffectual. In the 14th century, February 14 became a lovers' festival in Italy; in the 16th century, a day to send cards; and, lately, a time of roses and candle-lit dinners.

VANILLA

VERMOUTH
As an aperitif, followed by champagne and Hungarian Bull's Blood wine.

WORMWOOD
Used by Artemis, the goddess of fertility, and now an ingredient in absinthe. Mugwort, the common English wormwood, is also known as "the old man's plant" or "maiden's ruin."

X
X stands for a kiss, a powerful aphrodisiac.

YOHIMBE
Extracted from the bark of a tree in West Africa, yohimbe causes mice to ejaculate; evidence for its effects on humans is more elusive, but it is still popular in Africa and the West Indies.

ZOOS
Watching animals having sex.

Chez Aphrodite
–
Vermouth
–
Celery or broad bean soup
–
Scallops in oyster sauce
–
Truffles
–
Venison cooked in cider
–
Mushrooms, asparagus, or spinach
–
Chocolate almond gateau
–
Pineapple
–
Bananas and cream
–
Herring roes
–
Gorgonzola
–
Champagne

WORLD TABLE

Countries	1 PREGNANCY Average number of births per woman 2000	2 TEENAGE PREGNANCY Annual births per 100 15- to 19-year-olds 1995	3 CONTRACEPTION Percentage of women using modern methods 1998	4 INFERTILITY Percentage of couples with primary infertility 1995	5 CONDOM USE Percentage of couples 1990s
Afghanistan	5.9	15	–	5%	–
Albania	2.4	1	–	5%	–
Algeria	3.2	3	49%	3%	0.5%
Angola	6.1	24	–	12%	–
Argentina	2.5	6	–	3%	–
Armenia	2.6	6	–	–	–
Australia	1.8	2	72%	5%	4%
Austria	1.5	2	56%	5%	4%
Azerbaijan	2.4	2	–	–	–
Bahamas	1.8	–	60%	–	2%
Bahrain	3.7	–	30%	–	8%
Bangladesh	4.0	13	42%	4%	3%
Barbados	1.8	–	53%	–	7%
Belarus	1.8	3	42%	–	–
Belgium	1.6	1	75%	7%	5%
Belize	3.6	–	42%	–	2%
Benin	6.3	15	3%	3%	0.1%
Bhutan	5.1	–	19%	–	–
Bolivia	3.6	8	18%	3%	0.3%
Bosnia-Herzegovina	1.6	–	–	–	–
Botswana	3.1	–	32%	–	1%
Brazil	2.1	8	70%	2%	2%
Brunei	3.3	–	–	–	–
Bulgaria	1.7	6	–	6%	2%
Burkina Faso	6.5	17	4%	6%	1%
Burma	3.3	3	14%	5%	–
Burundi	6.3	6	1%	3%	0.1%
Cambodia	5.8	–	5%	–	–
Cameroon	5.6	14	7%	12%	1%
Canada	1.8	3	75%	7%	8%
Central African Rep.	5.1	16	3%	17%	–
Chad	5.1	19	1%	11%	–
Chile	2.4	6	–	3%	–
China	1.8	2	83%	5%	4%
Colombia	2.2	7	59%	2%	3%
Comoros	6.3	–	11%	–	–
Congo	4.8	15	–	21%	–
Congo, Dem. Rep.	6.4	23	2%	21%	0.5%
Costa Rica	2.8	9	65%	2%	16%
Côte-d'Ivoire	6.2	23	4%	10%	–
Croatia	1.6	–	–	–	–
Cuba	1.8	9	67%	6%	2%
Cyprus	2.2	–	–	–	–

 Sources: Col 1: Population Action International, United Nations and World Health Organization; Col 2: Population Action International, UNICEF, *The State of the World's Children* 1999; Col 3: Population Action International, United Nations and World Health Organization; Col 4: Population Action International; Col 5: UN, US Bureau of the Census;

6 AIDS Adults aged 15 to 49 living with HIV / AIDS 1997		7 MARRIAGE Legal minimum age in years 1996		8 DIVORCE Percentage of married couples who are divorced or separated 1997	9 HOMOSEXUALITY Legal status 1999	10 POPULATION 2000	Countries
numbers	percentages	men	women				
<100	<0.005%	–	–	0.5	illegal	26,668,251	Afghanistan
<100	0.01%	18	16	4.5	–	3,401,126	Albania
11,000	0.07%	–	–	1.4	illegal	31,787,647	Algeria
100,000	2.12%	–	–	0.6	illegal	11,486,729	Angola
120,000	0.69%	18	16	4.4	some protection	37,214,757	Argentina
<100	0.01%	18	18	2.0	illegal/men	3,396,184	Armenia
11,000	0.14%	18	18	8.15	some protection	18,950,108	Australia
7,500	0.18%	19	19	4.9	some protection	8,148,007	Austria
<100	<0.005%	–	–	2.8	illegal/men	7,955,772	Azerbaijan
6,200	3.77%	–	–	5.9	–	287,548	Bahamas
500	0.15%	–	–	1.1	illegal	641,539	Bahrain
21,000	0.03%	21	18	1.9	illegal	129,146,695	Bangladesh
4,200	2.89%	18	18	3.9	illegal	259,248	Barbados
9,000	0.17%	18	18	5.2	–	10,390,697	Belarus
7,200	0.14%	21	21	5.35	–	10,185,894	Belgium
2,100	1.89%	–	–	2.0	–	241,546	Belize
52,000	2.06%	–	–	3.2	illegal	6,516,630	Benin
<100	<0.005%	20	16	1.9	illegal/men	1,996,221	Bhutan
2,600	0.07%	16	14	5.5	–	8,139,180	Bolivia
750	0.04%	18	18	–	–	3,591,618	Bosnia-Herzegovina
190,000	25.10%	–	–	6.4	illegal/men	1,479,039	Botswana
570,000	0.63%	18	16	7.7	some protection	173,790,810	Brazil
300	0.20%	–	–	0.88	illegal	330,689	Brunei
300	0.01%	18	18	3.5	discrimination	8,155,828	Bulgaria
350,000	7.17%	20	17	1.1	–	11,892,029	Burkina Faso
440,000	1.79%	–	–	2.5	illegal/men	48,852,098	Burma
240,000	8.30%	–	–	2.65	illegal	5,930,805	Burundi
120,000	2.40%	20	18	–	–	11,918,865	Cambodia
310,000	4.89%	18	15	4.8	illegal	15,891,531	Cameroon
43,000	0.33%	16–18	16–18	6.55	some protection	31,330,255	Canada
170,000	10.77%	–	–	10.4	–	3,515,657	Central African Rep.
83,000	2.72%	–	–	–	unclear	7,760,252	Chad
15,000	0.20%	14	12	3.65	–	15,155,495	Chile
400,000	0.06%	22	20	0.6	–	1,256,167,701	China
72,000	0.36%	18	18	11.6	–	40,036,927	Colombia
400	0.14%	–	–	4.85	–	580,509	Comoros
95,000	7.78%	–	–	5.0	unclear	2,775,659	Congo
900,000	4.35%	21	21	3.4	–	51,987,773	Congo, Dem. Rep.
10,000	0.55%	18	18	–	–	3,743,677	Costa Rica
670,000	10.06%	–	–	4.5	–	16,190,105	Côte-d'Ivoire
300	0.01%	18	18	–	–	4,681,015	Croatia
1,400	0.02%	18	18	8.95	discrimination	11,139,412	Cuba
1,000	0.26%	18	16	1.5	discrimination	759,048	Cyprus

Col 6: WHO; Col 7: International Planned Parenthood Federation, Reproductive Rights, 1996; Col 8: US Bureau of the Census, International Database; Col 9: International Lesbian and Gay Association; Col 10: US Bureau of the Census, International Data Base, 1999

WORLD TABLE

Countries	1 PREGNANCY Average number of births per woman 2000	2 TEENAGE PREGNANCY Annual births per 100 15- to 19-year-olds 1995	3 CONTRACEPTION Percentage of women using modern methods 1998	4 INFERTILITY Percentage of couples with primary infertility 1995	5 CONDOM USE Percentage of couples 1990s
Czech Republic	1.8	5	45%	4%	19%
Denmark	1.7	1	72%	6%	22%
Djibouti	5.8	–	–	–	–
Dominican Republic	2.4	9	59%	5%	1%
Ecuador	2.6	8	46%	5%	1%
Egypt	3.8	7	46%	4%	2%
El Salvador	3.3	13	48%	2%	2%
Equatorial Guinea	4.9	–	–	–	–
Eritrea	–	–	4%	–	–
Estonia	1.9	–	56%	–	–
Ethiopia	6.4	17	3%	10%	0.1%
Fiji	2.7	–	40%	–	–
Finland	1.8	1	–	5%	32%
France	1.8	1	69%	6%	4%
Gabon	3.7	–	–	–	–
Gambia	6.9	–	7%	–	0.4%
Georgia	2.1	5	–	–	–
Germany	1.5	1	72%	4%	4%
Ghana	5.8	13	10%	3%	0.3%
Greece	1.5	–	–	–	–
Guatemala	4.0	12	27%	3%	1%
Guinea	5.5	24	1%	6%	–
Guinea Bissau	5.0	–	–	–	–
Guyana	2.1	–	–	–	3%
Haiti	5.2	5	13%	7%	0.5%
Honduras	3.8	13	41%	3%	3%
Hong Kong	1.5	1	80%	5%	26%
Hungary	1.8	4	60%	5%	4%
Iceland	1.8	–	–	–	–
India	3.0	6	37%	3%	5%
Indonesia	2.5	6	52%	7%	1%
Iran	5.9	9	45%	3%	6%
Iraq	5.8	5	10%	3%	1%
Ireland	1.8	–	–	–	–
Israel	2.7	2	–	6%	–
Italy	1.5	1	–	6%	13%
Jamaica	2.1	9	58%	7%	18%
Japan	1.6	0	53%	6%	48%
Jordan	4.6	5	38%	3%	1%
Kazakhstan	2.3	3	46%	–	–
Kenya	5.0	14	27%	7%	1%
Kirgistan	3.1	4	49%	–	–
Korea (North)	2.2	1	53%	2%	–

Sources: Col 1: Population Action International, United Nations and World Health Organization; Col 2: Population Action International, UNICEF, *The State of the World's Children 1999*; Col 3: Population Action International, United Nations and World Health Organization; Col 4: Population Action International; Col 5: UN, US Bureau of the Census;

AIDS Adults aged 15 to 49 living with HIV / AIDS 1997		MARRIAGE Legal minimum age in years 1996		DIVORCE Percentage of married couples who are divorced or separated 1997	HOMOSEXUALITY Legal status 1999	POPULATION 2000	Countries
numbers	percentages	men	women				
2,000	0.04%	18	18	–	–	10,283,762	Czech Republic
3,100	0.12%	18	18	6.65	some protection	5,374,554	Denmark
32,000	10.30%	–	–	–	illegal	454,294	Djibouti
81,000	5.17%	18	18	14.6	–	8,261,536	Dominican Republic
18,000	0.28%	18	18	0.7	some protection	12,782,161	Ecuador
8,100	0.03%	18	16	1.5	–	68,494,584	Egypt
18,000	0.58%	21	21	15.1	–	5,925,374	El Salvador
2,300	1.21%	–	–	3.75	–	477,763	Equatorial Guinea
49,000	3.17%	–	–	5.75	–	4,142,481	Eritrea
<100	0.01%	18	18	8.6	–	1,398,140	Estonia
2,500,000	9.31%	18	15	7.0	illegal	60,967,436	Ethiopia
260	0.06%	–	–	1.1	some protection	823,376	Fiji
500	0.02%	18	18	6.15	some protection	5,164,825	Finland
110,000	0.37%	18	18	5.15	some protection	59,128,187	France
22,000	4.25%	18	15	3.15	unclear	1,244,192	Gabon
13,000	2.24%	nil	nil	3.7	unclear	1,381,496	Gambia
<100	<0.005%	18	18	4.3	some protection	5,034,051	Georgia
35,000	0.08%	18	18	4.55	some protection	82,081,365	Germany
200,000	2.38%	21	21	7.35	–	19,271,744	Ghana
7,500	0.14%	18	18	1.3	–	10,750,705	Greece
27,000	0.52%	18	18	6.1	–	12,669,576	Guatemala
70,000	2.09%	18	17	1.0	–	7,610,869	Guinea
11,000	2.25%	18	15	–	unclear	1,263,341	Guinea Bissau
10,000	2.13%	18	18	2.85	illegal/men	703,399	Guyana
180,000	5.17%	18	18	6.7	–	6,991,589	Haiti
41,000	1.46%	21	21	2.6	–	6,130,135	Honduras
3,100	0.08%	–	–	1.9	–	6,966,929	Hong Kong
2,000	0.04%	18	18	15.55	–	10,167,182	Hungary
200	0.14%	18	18	4.3	some protection	274,141	Iceland
4,100,000	0.82%	20	18	0.55	illegal/men	1,017,645,163	India
51,000	0.05%	19	16	2.6	–	219,266,557	Indonesia
1,000	<0.005%	–	–	0.5	illegal	65,865,302	Iran
300	<0.005%	18	18	0.85	–	23,150,926	Iraq
1,700	0.09%	21	21	2.45	some protection	3,647,348	Ireland
2,100	0.07%	–	16	–	some protection	5,851,913	Israel
90,000	0.31%	18	18	1.8	–	56,686,568	Italy
14,000	0.99%	16	16	0.8	illegal/men	2,668,740	Jamaica
6,800	0.01%	18	16	2.6	–	126,434,470	Japan
660	0.02%	18	17	1.0	–	4,700,843	Jordan
2,500	0.03%	–	–	7.2	–	16,816,150	Kazakhstan
1,600,000	11.64%	18	18	4.5	illegal/men	29,250,541	Kenya
<100	<0.005%	–	–	4.5	–	4,584,341	Kirgistan
<100	<0.005%	–	–	–	–	21,687,550	Korea (North)

Col 6: WHO; Col 7: International Planned Parenthood Federation, Reproductive Rights, 1996; Col 8: US Bureau of the Census, International Database; Col 9: International Lesbian and Gay Association; Col 10: US Bureau of the Census, International Data Base, 1999

WORLD TABLE

Countries	1 PREGNANCY Average number of births per woman 2000	2 TEENAGE PREGNANCY Annual births per 100 15- to 19-year-olds 1995	3 CONTRACEPTION Percentage of women using modern methods 1998	4 INFERTILITY Percentage of couples with primary infertility 1995	5 CONDOM USE Percentage of couples 1990s
Korea (South)	1.7	1	70%	2%	10%
Kuwait	3.7	–	32%	–	2%
Laos	5.4	5	15%	5%	–
Latvia	1.9	4	39%	–	–
Lebanon	3.0	3	37%	3%	–
Lesotho	3.9	–	19%	–	1%
Liberia	6.0	23	5%	4%	<1%
Libya	6.0	11	26%	3%	–
Lithuania	1.9	3	40%	–	–
Luxembourg	1.7	–	–	–	–
Macedonia	1.8	–	–	–	–
Madagascar	6.3	16	10%	10%	1%
Malawi	6.9	17	14%	10%	2%
Malaysia	3.3	3	31%	4%	6%
Mali	6.9	20	5%	8%	<1%
Malta	1.8	–	–	–	–
Marshall Islands	6.6	–	18%	–	–
Mauritania	6.5	13	1%	6%	0.1%
Mauritius	2.1	–	49%	–	11%
Mexico	2.8	8	58%	3%	2%
Moldova	2.1	4	50%	–	–
Mongolia	3.9	4	25%	5%	–
Morocco	3.1	4	42%	3%	1%
Mozambique	5.8	13	5%	14%	–
Namibia	6.0	–	26%	–	0.3%
Nepal	4.7	10	26%	6%	0.5%
Netherlands	1.5	1	76%	5%	8%
New Zealand	1.8	4	72%	5%	8%
Nicaragua	3.5	15	45%	3%	3%
Niger	7.0	22	5%	9%	<1%
Nigeria	6.0	15	4%	8%	0.4%
Norway	1.5	2	69%	5%	14%
Oman	6.2	12	18%	3%	1%
Pakistan	5.9	6	13%	4%	3%
Panama	2.6	9	58%	3%	2%
Papua New Guinea	4.1	2	20%	5%	–
Paraguay	3.9	9	41%	3%	3%
Peru	2.6	6	41%	3%	3%
Philippines	2.9	3	28%	2%	1%
Poland	1.8	3	–	3%	14%
Portugal	1.5	3	33%	5%	6%
Qatar	2.9	–	29%	–	2%
Romania	1.8	4	15%	6%	4%

Sources: Col 1: Population Action International, United Nations and World Health Organization; Col 2: Population Action International, UNICEF, *The State of the World's Children 1999*; Col 3: Population Action International, United Nations and World Health Organization; Col 4: Population Action International; Col 5: UN, US Bureau of the Census;

6 AIDS Adults aged 15 to 49 living with HIV / AIDS 1997		7 MARRIAGE Legal minimum age in years 1996		8 DIVORCE Percentage of married couples who are divorced or separated 1997	9 HOMOSEXUALITY Legal status 1999	10 POPULATION 2000	Countries
numbers	percentages	men	women				
3,100	0.01%	18	16	1.0	–	47,350,529	Korea (South)
1,100	0.12%	nil	nil	1.0	illegal/men	2,067,728	Kuwait
1,000	0.04%	nil	nil	2.2	illegal/men	5,556,821	Laos
<100	0.01%	18	18	9.2	–	2,326,689	Latvia
1,500	0.09%	–	–	0.6	illegal	3,619,971	Lebanon
82,000	8.35%	–	–	3.9	–	2,166,520	Lesotho
42,000	3.65%	16	16	9.4	illegal	3,089,980	Liberia
1,400	0.05%	20	20	1.8	illegal	5,114,032	Libya
<100	0.01%	18	18	8.3	–	3,571,552	Lithuania
300	0.14%	18	18	3.95	some protection	432,577	Luxembourg
<100	0.01%	18	18	–	–	2,035,044	Macedonia
8,200	0.12%	18	18	4.75	–	15,294,535	Madagascar
670,000	14.92%	nil	nil	7.6	illegal	10,154,299	Malawi
66,000	0.62%	–	–	0.85	illegal/men	21,820,143	Malaysia
84,000	1.67%	21	18	1.3	unclear	10,750,686	Mali
200	0.11%	–	–	1.1	–	383,285	Malta
–	–	–	–	1.1	illegal/men	68,088	Marshall Islands
5,900	0.52%	–	–	6.5	illegal	2,660,155	Mauritania
500	0.08%	18	18	2.5	illegal	1,196,172	Mauritius
180,000	0.35%	18	18	1.9	–	102,026,691	Mexico
2,500	0.11%	18	18	4.5	–	4,466,758	Moldova
<100	0.01%	18	18	2.2	–	2,654,572	Mongolia
5,000	0.03%	18	15	3.4	illegal	30,205,387	Morocco
1,200,000	14.17%	–	–	2.6	illegal/men	19,614,345	Mozambique
150,000	19.94%	21	18	5.5	illegal/men	1,674,116	Namibia
25,000	0.24%	18	18	1.7	illegal/men	24,920,211	Nepal
14,000	0.17%	18	18	2.75	some protection	15,878,304	Netherlands
1,300	0.07%	20	20	9.15	some protection	3,697,850	New Zealand
4,100	0.19%	15	14	–	illegal	4,850,976	Nicaragua
61,000	1.45%	–	–	2.9	–	10,260,316	Niger
2,200,000	4.12%	16	16	2.0	illegal/men	117,170,948	Nigeria
1,300	0.06%	18	18	4.45	some protection	4,455,707l	Norway
1,200	0.11%	–	–	3.05	illegal	2,532,556	Oman
62,000	0.09%	–	–	0.7	illegal	141,145,344	Pakistan
8,800	0.61%	16	15	8.6	–	2,821,085	Panama
4,200	0.19%	18	16	4.0	illegal/men	4,811,939	Papua New Guinea
3,100	0.13%	14	12	1.4	–	5,579,503	Paraguay
71,000	0.56%	16	14	6.3	–	27,135,689	Peru
23,000	0.06%	18	18	1.8	–	80,961,430	Philippines
12,000	0.06%	21	18	2.8	–	38,644,184	Poland
35,000	0.69%	18	18	2.2	–	9,902,147	Portugal
300	0.09%	–	–	–	illegal	749,542	Qatar
1,000	0.01%	18	16	2.95	discrimination	22,291,200	Romania

Col 6: WHO; Col 7: International Planned Parenthood Federation, Reproductive Rights, 1996; Col 8: US Bureau of the Census, International Database; Col 9: International Lesbian and Gay Association; Col 10: US Bureau of the Census, International Data Base, 1999

WORLD TABLE

Countries	1 PREGNANCY Average number of births per woman 2000	2 TEENAGE PREGNANCY Annual births per 100 15- to 19-year-olds 1995	3 CONTRACEPTION Percentage of women using modern methods 1998	4 INFERTILITY Percentage of couples with primary infertility 1995	5 CONDOM USE Percentage of couples 1990s
Russia	1.8	4	–	–	–
Rwanda	7.6	6	13%	10%	0.2%
Saudi Arabia	6.4	12	–	3%	–
Senegal	5.7	16	8%	4%	0.4%
Seychelles	2.0	–	–	–	–
Sierra Leone	5.6	21	–	10%	–
Singapore	1.8	1	73%	5%	24%
Slovakia	1.8	4	41%	5%	21%
Slovenia	1.6	–	–	–	–
Solomon Islands	4.8	–	–	–	–
Somalia	6.5	21	–	10%	–
South Africa	4.2	7	48%	5%	1%
Spain	1.5	1	38%	4%	12%
Sri Lanka	1.9	3	44%	4%	2%
Sudan	5.5	9	7%	9%	0.1%
Suriname	2.5	–	–	–	–
Swaziland	5.9	–	17%	–	1%
Sweden	1.8	1	71%	5%	25%
Switzerland	1.6	1	65%	5%	8%
Syria	6.0	11	28%	3%	1%
Taiwan	1.8	2	–	5%	14%
Tajikistan	4.1	3	–	–	–
Tanzania	5.9	13	13%	10%	1%
Thailand	1.9	5	72%	2%	1%
Togo	6.5	13	7%	10%	0.4%
Trinidad & Tobago	2.1	–	44%	–	12%
Tunisia	2.3	2	51%	7%	1%
Turkey	2.8	4	35%	2%	7%
Turkmenistan	3.4	–	–	–	–
Uganda	6.7	22	8%	10%	<1%
Ukraine	1.8	4	–	–	–
United Arab Emirates	4.2	–	44%	–	–
United Kingdom	1.8	3	82%	6%	16%
United States	2.1	6	67%	6%	11%
Uruguay	2.3	6	–	3%	–
Uzbekistan	3.4	3	51%	–	–
Venezuela	2.7	10	40%	2%	5%
Vietnam	2.8	2	44%	2%	1%
Western Sahara	6.6	–	–	–	–
Yemen	6.7	10	10%	2%	0.1%
Yugoslavia	–	4	–	5%	2%
Zambia	6.3	14	14%	14%	2%
Zimbabwe	4.1	10	42%	10%	1%

 Sources: Col 1: Population Action International, United Nations and World Health Organization; Col 2: Population Action International, UNICEF, *The State of the World's Children 1999*; Col 3: Population Action International, United Nations and World Health Organization; Col 4: Population Action International; Col 5: UN, US Bureau of the Census;

6 AIDS Adults aged 15 to 49 living with HIV / AIDS 1997		7 MARRIAGE Legal minimum age in years 1996		8 DIVORCE Percentage of married couples who are divorced or separated 1997	9 HOMOSEXUALITY Legal status 1999	10 POPULATION 2000	Countries
numbers	percentages	men	women				
40,000	0.05%	18	18	7.2	–	145,904,542	Russia
350,000	12.75%	21	21	6.1	–	8,336,995	Rwanda
1,100	0.01%	–	–	–	illegal	22,245,751	Saudi Arabia
72,000	1.77%	20	16	4.1	illegal	10,390,296	Senegal
–	–	–	–	3.15	illegal/men	79,672	Seychelles
64,000	3.17%	21	18	–	illegal/men	5,509,263	Sierra Leone
3,100	0.15%	–	–	1.2	illegal/men	3,571,710	Singapore
<100	<0.005%	18	18	–	–	5,401,134	Slovakia
<100	0.01%	18	18	3.45	some protection	1,970,056	Slovenia
–	–	–	–	1.25	illegal	470,000	Solomon Islands
11,000	0.25%	–	–	–	illegal/men	7,433,922	Somalia
2,800,000	12.91%	–	–	3.55	some protection	43,981,758	South Africa
120,000	0.57%	18	18	0.4	some protection	39,208,236	Spain
6,700	0.07%	21	21	4.9	illegal/men	19,355,053	Sri Lanka
140,000	0.99%	–	–	2.7	illegal	35,530,371	Sudan
2,700	1.17%	–	–	–	discrimination	434,093	Suriname
81,000	18.50%	–	–	0.7	illegal	1,004,072	Swaziland
3,000	0.07%	18	18	6.9	some protection	8,938,559	Sweden
12,000	0.32%	–	–	5.7	some protection	7,288,715	Switzerland
800	0.01%	–	–	0.5	illegal	17,758,925	Syria
–	–	–	–	3.2	–	22,319,222	Taiwan
<100	<0.005%	18	18	2.9	illegal/men	6,194,373	Tajikistan
1,400,000	9.42%	18	18	7.3	illegal/men	31,962,769	Tanzania
770,000	2.23%	17	17	2.7	–	61,163,833	Thailand
160,000	8.52%	21	21	3.4	illegal	5,262,611	Togo
6,700	0.94%	18	18	3.2	illegal	1,086,908	Trinidad & Tobago
2,200	0.04%	20	20	1.1	illegal	9,645,499	Tunisia
2,000	0.01%	17	15	1.0	–	66,620,120	Turkey
<100	0.01%	–	–	2.8	unclear	4,435,507	Turkmenistan
870,000	9.51%	21	21	6.9	illegal/men	23,451,687	Uganda
110,000	0.43%	18	18	6.5	–	49,506,779	Ukraine
2,400	0.18%	–	–	–	illegal	2,386,472	United Arab Emirates
25,000	0.09%	16	16	4.8	discrimination	59,247,439	United Kingdom
810,000	0.76%	14–21	14–21	12.0	some protection	274,943,496	United States
5,200	0.33%	21	21	3.6	–	3,332,782	Uruguay
<100	<0.005%	–	–	3.0	illegal/men	24,422,518	Uzbekistan
81,000	0.69%	16	16	5.4	some protection	23,595,822	Venezuela
86,000	0.22%	20	18	1.2	–	78,349,503	Vietnam
–	–	–	–	–	–	244,943	Western Sahara
900	0.01%	15	15	2.2	illegal	17,521,085	Yemen
5,000	0.10%	18	18	–	–	10,529,507	Yugoslavia
730,000	19.07%	21	21	9.2	illegal/men	9,872,007	Zambia
1,400,000	25.84%	18	18	6.0	illegal/men	11,272,013	Zimbabwe

Col 6: WHO; Col 7: International Planned Parenthood Federation, Reproductive Rights, 1996; Col 8: US Bureau of the Census, International Database; Col 9: International Lesbian and Gay Association; Col 10: US Bureau of the Census, International Data Base, 1999

GLOSSARY

ABORTION: Natural or induced expulsion of the products of conception, terminating a pregnancy.

APHRODISIACS: Any drugs, food, drinks, plants, animal parts, smells, or objects which are believed to arouse sexual desire.

ASEXUAL REPRODUCTION: Self-replication, so the offspring carry the sole parent's genes. This may be a bacteria dividing into two, or a female plant or animal producing an identical female offspring. Most species of animals which exhibit asexual reproduction can also reproduce sexually.

ALPHA MALE OR FEMALE: Dominant, successful individual.

BESTIALITY: Sexual intercourse between humans and animals of other species.

BISEXUAL: A person who has significant sexual and romantic attractions to members of both the same and the other gender.

BONDAGE: The act of restraining a person with rope, handcuffs or other physical means during a sexual encounter between dominant and submissive partners.

CELIBACY: Not having sexual intercourse for a long time.

CHASTITY: Never having had sexual intercourse.

CHROMOSOMES: Paired thread-like structures, located in the nucleii of cells carrying genetic information in the form of DNA.

CIRCUMCISION: The surgical removal of the prepuce (foreskin) from the penis.

CLONE: A plant or animal having exactly the same genetic composition as the original from which it was produced.

CONSUMMATE: A marriage has been consummated when the couple have achieved penetrative sexual intercourse.

CONTRACEPTION: Any method used to prevent pregnancy.

CROSS-DRESSER/TRANSVESTITE: A person who enjoys wearing the clothes usually reserved for use by the opposite gender, but has no desire to change their sex permanently. The majority are male and are attracted to women.

CUNNILINGUS: Sexual stimulation of the clitoris and/or vagina with another person's tongue.

CYBERSEX: Electronic sex over the internet: chat lines, verbal cybersex in discussion groups, video interactions, sex suits allowing a person to physically interact with another.

DNA: Deoxyribonucleic acids, molecules that make up chromosomes.

EROGENOUS ZONES: Parts of the body that when stimulated lead to sexual arousal. Traditionally genitals and nipples, but can include any part of the body.

EROTICA: Objects, pictures, books, films, performances, that excite sexual arousal. They are not necessarily pornographic.

ESTROGENS: Female sex hormones produced in the ovary that control development of female physical characteristics and sexual functioning.

FELLATIO: Sexual stimulation of the penis with another person's mouth.

FEMALE GENITAL EXCISION (FGE): also known as female genital mutilation (FGM), although excision is the more accurate medical term. There are four types of FGE: Sunna (removal of the tip of the clitoris); Clitoridectomy (removal of entire clitoris); Pharaonic, where both labia and clitoris are removed and the orifice is sewn up (and again after each delivery, on divorce and on the death of her husband); and the most extensive, Type IV, which is rarely practiced, which involves enlarging the vaginal opening by cutting the perineum.

GAY: Homosexual man or woman.

GENES: The units of DNA on the chromosomes that determine a person's inherited characteristics.

HERMAPHRODITE: One who has both a penis and a vagina.

HETEROSEXUALITY: Sexual attraction, interest or activity between members of the opposite gender.

HOMOPHOBIA: Originally an irrational fear of sexual attraction to the same sex, and now used to mean anti-homosexual.

HOMOSEXUALITY: Sexual attraction, interest or activity between members of the same sex.

HUMAN IMMUNODEFICIENCY VIRUS (HIV): A virus passed from person to person by exchange of body fluid, usually blood. After some months or years it leads to Acquired Immune Deficiency Syndrome (AIDS), or an AIDS-related disease.

HUMAN PAPILLOMA VIRUS: A virus which causes warts, usually passed by sexual contact, and some strains are associated with an increased incidence of cervical cancer.

HYPOTHALAMUS: An area in the center of the brain which influences the pituitary gland, which in turn influences the testes and ovary by the release of sex hormones.

IMPOTENCE: Inability of a man to achieve or maintain a penile erection sufficiently long to have penetrative sex. Primary impotence: has never had the ability. Secondary impotence: loss of the ability (more common).

INFERTILITY: Inability to achieve a pregnancy.

INTERSEX: Person born with chromosomal or external genital configurations that do not neatly fit into either of the two sexual classifications which society expects. Examples are an unusually large clitoris, micropenis, ambiguous genitals; chromosome abnormalities like Klinefelter's, and hormonal causes such as adrenal hyperplasia, androgen insensitivity, testicular feminization. (Traditionally if a boy had a penis of less than 2.5cm long, he was made into a girl; if a girl had a clitoris of greater than 0.9cm it would be reduced, independent of the cause. Gender surgery was always done in the first two years, but current thinking is to delay and make a more measured decision.)

IUCD: Intra-uterine contraceptive device. A small plastic and metal object which is inserted through the vagina into the uterus to prevent implantation of a fertilized ovum. It has to be changed at intervals of several years.

LABIA: Folds of skin forming the outer and inner edges, or lips, of the vagina.

LESBIAN: Homosexual female.

MAMMOPLASTY: Surgical alteration of the shape of a breast.

MASTURBATION: Sexual self-stimulation.

MENARCHE: The time of a girl's first menstruation.

MONOGAMOUS: Sexual relationship between only two people at one time.

NOCTURNAL EMISSION: Male ejaculation during sleep ("wet dream").

OBSCENITY: Behavior, speech, or object (e.g. film or book) deemed offensive in law.

ORGASM: The climax of sexual excitement. In the male it involves spasmodic contractions of the body and ejaculation of semen from the penis. In the female it involves similar spasmodic contractions of the pelvic sex organs.

ORO-GENITAL CONTACT: *see* Cunnilingus, Fellatio

PEDERAST: A person who has sexual activity with young boys.

PEDOPHILE: A person who has sexual activity with children of either sex.

PETTING: Sexual activity including deep kissing and touching of erogenous zones, which may lead to orgasm, but does not involve penetrative sexual intercourse.

PHEROMES: Androstenol and androstenone are steroids present in human armpit perspiration, the smell of which has some (mostly still unknown) influence on sexual behavior.

PIMP: Person living off the earnings of one or more prostitutes.

PITUITARY: A small structure attached to the brain that produces several different hormones, including sex hormones controlling the ovary and testes.

POLYANDRY: The marriage between one woman and two or more men.

POLYGAMY: The marriage between one man and two or more women.

PORNOGRAPHY: There is no universally accepted definition of pornography, but in general it refers to material that is predominantly sexually explicit and intended primarily for the purpose of sexual arousal.

PROSTITUTION: The provision of sexual services for a reward or money.

RAPE: Any kind of act of sexual penetration committed by any means on a person who does not consent.

SEXUAL HARASSMENT: Any type of unwanted verbal or physical sexual advance.

SEXUAL IDENTITY: The belief that a person has as to his or her own masculinity or femininity.

SEXUAL ORIENTATION: A person's preference for homosexual, heterosexual, or bisexual relationships.

SEXUAL REPRODUCTION: Male and female genes mix to produce offspring which inherit half their genes from each parent.

SEXUALLY-TRANSMITTED INFECTIONS (STI): Infections that can be transmitted sexually may be bacterial: gonorrhea, non-specific urethritis, syphilis, chancroid, granuloma inguinale, lymphogranuloma venereum; micro parasites: chlamydia, trichomonas; yeasts: monilia or thrush; or viral: herpes, HIV, hepatitis B, human papilloma virus.

SIBLING: A brother or sister.

SODOMY: Legally defined as the sexual act of putting a penis into a man's or woman's anus or mouth; in some countries refers also to sex with animals.

STALKING: Wilful and repeatedly following and harassing another person, placing that person in fear for their safety.

STATUTORY RAPE: Sexual intercourse with a person who is under the "age of consent."

STERILITY: The inability of a woman to become pregnant, and of a man to produce adequate sperm cells to cause pregnancy.

TESTOSTERONE: A hormone produced in the testes, responsible for male sexual characteristics and sexual functioning.

TRANSGENDER: An umbrella term for having a self-image or identity not traditionally associated with the person's biological maleness or femaleness. Transgender individuals cross or transcend culturally defined categories of gender, and there are many different types, which include transsexual, transgenderist, transvestite and intersex.

TRANSGENDERIST: Person who lives in the other gender role without seeking surgery but may take hormones.

TRANSSEXUAL: Transsexuals have the strong feeling, often from childhood onwards, of having been born the wrong sex, contrary to their genetic, physical and hormonal gender. They feel their core gender is not that of their assigned sex, and may seek medical and surgical assistance for reassignment. Investigation of genetics, gonads, genitalia or hormone level of transsexuals has not, so far, produced any results that explain their status. Some studies indicate a possible slight brain difference, but this requires further investigation.

TRANSVESTITE/CROSS-DRESSER: Person who enjoys wearing the clothes usually reserved for use by the opposite gender, but has no desire to change their sex permanently. The majority are men and are attracted to women.

TUBAL LIGATION: Operation on a woman in which the fallopian tubes are cut. This causes sterility by stopping the sperm cells from reaching the ovum.

VASECTOMY: Operation on a man to block the passage (vas deferens) that allows sperm cells to travel down from the testis.

VIRGIN: Male or female, who has not had penetrative sexual intercourse. An intact hymen indicates a female's virginity. Hymen repairs are possible. The hymen may be virtually absent or stretched and the female still be a virgin.

COMMENTARY ON THE MAPS

THE SEX DRIVE

Life has existed on earth for 3,000 million years, reproducing asexually until about 2,000 million years ago, when some plants changed over to reproducing sexually. Why and how this change evolved is unclear, but there are advantages (as well as disadvantages) to both forms of reproduction. Today, sexual and asexual reproduction exist side by side. Out of the 1.5 million named species on earth (out of somewhere between 10 million and 100 million that probably exist), about 15,000 species of animals can reproduce asexually, 1,000 are obliged to do so. Different species of plants reproduce sexually and asexually; most bacteria and fungi reproduce asexually.

Sex in the animal kingdom, even among primates, is diverse. Some animals copulate frequently with a huge number of different partners, while others are monogamous for life. The key seems to be the survival advantage to offspring offered by different mating patterns.

Part One SEXUALITY

PUBERTY

At the moment of conception, the genetic decision is made as to whether the fetus will be male (chromosome XY) or female (XX). By six weeks from conception there are already observable differences: the Y chromosome causes miniature testes to form, which by seven to eight weeks already produce testosterone for the development of male sexual organs. Most of the time genetic and hormonal sexual development are in tandem, but in rare instances the hormone environment can contradict the chromosomal blueprint, causing gender confusion at birth (see **Transgender** pp 24–25).

Rites of passage marking the transition from childhood to adulthood typically occur for girls within the family when the first menstruation appears, when they are taught taboos and their role in society. Rites for boys usually occur about one year after sexual maturity, in community gatherings, often requiring the performance of tasks and experiencing of hardships, even mutilation. These rituals are found less often in modern societies.

There are considerable variations in size, shape, color, smell, taste, sensitivity and texture of the sexual organs – between individuals, between ethnic groups, between the young and the old, between men and women – which often cause unwarranted concerns, especially during puberty.

FIRST ENCOUNTERS

Sexual activity is observed from birth with babies touching their genitals, followed by children's intense curiosity in their own bodies and those of the opposite sex, and in how babies are made. During the teen years there is a wide diversity and continuum from no sexual activity to penetrative sex.

Research in the USA shows that sexual activity among teenagers climbed steadily from 1970 but then fell 11 percent during the 1990s. Sexually-active teenagers are more likely to use contraceptives than in the past, with condom use increasing the most dramatically, leading to fewer teen pregnancies in every state.

In the UK the trend is in the opposite direction. While in 1957 only 1 percent of girls and boys had sex before 16 years of age, this rose to 25 percent of boys and 20 percent of girls in 1997, with one in every 100 girls aged 13–15 becoming pregnant. Research from 53 rich and poor countries indicates that many teenage girls feel coerced into having sex. In the USA, 40 percent of girls who had sex before 15 said they were forced into it.

Studies from Latin America and elsewhere show that girls with fewer years of schooling are far more likely to have sex in their teens than those with 10 or more years of schooling.

SEXUAL PRACTICES

Except in a very few countries, we have no idea what people do in bed. Even in careful, representative surveys, the accuracy of data can be questionable, as respondents may report an exaggerated frequency of sex, or an underestimation for masturbation, cross-dressing, or same-sex activity.

Some surveys only interview sexually-active people, so the views of the sexually-inactive are not represented, although they form a substantial segment of society. For example, in a national survey in the USA, 30 percent of men and 28 percent of women were celibate or had sex only a few times each year. Internet surveys also are far from typical, as they tend to attract mostly male respondents, with an average age of under 25 years.

Even the definition of "sex" causes confusion. In the USA in 1999, two thirds of respondents in a survey reported in a medical journal believed that oral-genital contact did not constitute "having sex," and one in five thought the same about anal intercourse.

What is clear is that sexual practices, in all their variety, are universal. In the UK, the average person spends three and a half years of their life eating, two and a half years talking on phone, two weeks kissing and has sex 2,580 times with five different people.

Married or not, people have significantly less sex as they get older, although decline in frequency of sex has more to do with the length of marriage or the relationship than with age. The frequency of sex varies according to culture. Sex after the age of 40 is significantly lower in some parts of Asia compared with the West. In India, for example, many couples abstain from sex at 50, or when a woman has a married daughter or becomes a grandmother.

Sex tends to keep people healthy. The doctor who

replied to the patient's question, "Will I live longer if I give up drinking and sex?" with "No, but it will seem like it" may have been right all along.

HOMOSEXUALITY

Homosexuality is evident early in life. So far biomedical research has failed to show a cause, although research into genetics, hormones and upbringing is continuing. Research in Brazil, Peru, the Philippines, and the USA has shown that lesbian sexuality and identity eventually emerge, regardless of culture.

Various theories have been put forward. Kinsey and others found that homosexual men (but not women) have a later birth order, a greater number of older brothers, an earlier onset of puberty, and a lower body weight.

However, many would argue that research into the cause of homosexuality should not be done at all, as it assumes that homosexuality is an illness or undesirable deviance from the heterosexual norm, and should be "cured."

Legislation is slowly changing, but homosexuality is still illegal in about 50 countries, and for men only in a further 50 countries. Even in countries which have decriminalized homosexuality, gays and lesbians are often still subject to harassment, discrimination, violence, and persecution by the government, police, employers, and by the population at large.

Studies in Europe show more than one quarter of lesbians and gays report being victims of violent hate crimes. Same-sex couples requesting one bed in US guest houses were granted significantly fewer reservations than opposite-sex couples.

Young homosexuals also suffer. In the USA, while 19 percent of respondents to a survey on an internet site for young homosexuals, bisexuals, and transgendered youth had taken a date of the same gender to the high-school prom, 74 percent said they would like to do so.

Gays and lesbians with a well-founded fear of persecution because of their homosexuality can claim asylum under the 1951 UN Convention relating to the Status of Refugees and its 1967 Protocol. But, in practice, only a small number of countries recognize and accept lesbian and gay refugees.

In 1994 the UN Human Rights Committee ruled that "sex" in the clauses on non-discrimination should be taken as including "sexual orientation." The European Court of Human Rights has ruled that laws criminalizing consensual sex between adult men are in breach of the privacy protections of the European Convention on Human Rights. Amnesty International has called on governments to protect the human rights of lesbian, gay, bisexual, and transgendered people.

TRANSGENDER

Many people think there are just two sexes, male and female. But this has never been the case: The *I Ching*, the oldest Chinese classic, held that within the human body there are both *yin* (female) and *yang* (male) essences. Nature is dependent upon a balance of these elements. Similarly, one of the major teachings of Hinduism is that every man and woman contains within him or herself both male and female principles. Al-Bukhari, the famous ninth-century commentator on the Koran, devoted an entire section to "men who wish to resemble women, and women who wish to resemble men." Cross dressing is also common in Hindu mythology.

Such is also the case today. Babies are sometimes born with chromosomes other than XX (female) or XY (male), such as XO, XXX, XXY or XXXY. Very rarely there are true hermaphrodites who have both male and female sex organs.

Likewise, gender, social sex role, and sexual orientation are not simple cases of "either/or." People who are intersexed or transsexual are neither exactly male nor exactly female, with respect to their genes, bodies, hormones, behavior, sexual preferences, or by their inherent belief of their own gender.

Research on what factors influence gender identity is inconclusive. Biological factors (hormonal, genetic) and psychosocial factors (culture, upbringing) probably interact.

Research in the USA shows that there have not been any significant or profound psychological effects on children whose parent has undergone gender re-assignment; and that the sexual orientation of children of gay or transsexual parents is unaffected by that of the parent.

Part Two MATING

SEX APPEAL

Fashions in the sex appeal of physical appearance change, as do fashions in clothes. In industrialized societies men would judge the buxom women painted by Michelangelo as too fat, and women are becoming attracted to less muscular, gentler-looking men.

Some societies appreciate beauty but are wary of its potentially disruptive effect, hence the Chinese proverb: "Ugly wives are treasures above price."

Power and money have always attracted. Research in the UK has shown that men and women are more likely to look twice at a potential partner with a pension.

Sexual feelings can be aroused by the appeal of parts of the body, such as breasts or toes, or from a wide variety of objects, such as women's underwear or rubber garments. Such feelings are generally referred to as sexual fetishisms.

Plastic surgery is becoming an increasingly popular way of trying to enhance physical attractiveness. In the USA, the most common plastic surgery procedure for men and women is liposuction. The next most common procedures for women are breast augmentation, eyelid surgery, facelifts, and chemical peels, and for men eyelid surgery, nose reshaping, breast reduction, and facelifts. Currently, nine percent of all cosmetic procedures are performed on men.

The future of constructed beauty lies not under the knife but in the laboratory, however. It is predicted that by 2020 we will be able to replace 96 percent of our body by creating new cells in the laboratory from existing cells – a form of personalized mini-cloning. By 2020 it should be possible to have a new face or new skin, and by 2030 a fully-working replacement body part. In theory, everything will be changeable, to fit personal needs and tastes.

DATING

Difficulty in finding a compatible mate leads some people to turn to dating services and "lonely-hearts columns." In 1999 Tokyo now had 5,000 agencies; in 1997 the Association of British Introduction Agencies represented 781,000 single women and 1,268,000 single men between the ages of 20 and 24 years. In almost 4,000 personal ads from men and women in 10 national magazines across China from 1984 to 1995, the most desirable love-match characteristics asked for were qualities such as a caring, compassionate, or romantic nature.

The most modern form of dating is on internet. Cyber-dating is mostly used by men looking for women and, as a result, women get about 50 times more replies to their personal advertisements than do men. Also, prostitution is moving from the streets to on-line dating agencies.

Hundreds of thousands of people engage in virtual sex in cyberspace every day – whereby two people (at minimum) "talk" each other through sex on an internet keyboard, with masturbation to orgasm.

Male homosexuals have far more casual partners than do lesbians. Lesbians tend to have sex with women with whom they already have a close friendship.

CHOOSE YOUR PARTNER

It may come as a surprise to many to realize that most marriages in the world are still arranged, and that in most cases parents make wise and considered choices for their children.

Worldwide, when couples choose their own partners, both men and women rate attraction, dependability, maturity, and a pleasing disposition as the top four qualities. Within a culture, men and women tend to value the same qualities, although there is some difference between cultures. Chastity is low on the list, but is still rated higher by men than women, and it shows the largest single cultural difference.

Both sexes want healthy and successful partners who will perpetuate their genes. **The Sex Drive** (pp 12–13) outlines the "selfish gene" theory that the choice of mate is based on maximizing reproductive possibility. Thus,

women choose "dads not cads" to ensure many years of protection for their offspring. Men choose younger, more fertile women.

There may be other influences at play, such as the Chinese belief in compatibility or incompatibility between various birth years in a 12-year lunar cycle. The Japanese put great store by ABO blood groups, which are widely believed to affect personality and employment prospects, and are therefore vital considerations in choosing a mate.

In China, one in six men, or 110 million, will not find a mate. There are 1.8 young, unmarried men to every woman, due to consequences of the one-child policy; the ratio is reversed in the older population. Everywhere in the world older women have a restricted choice of partner because there are fewer older men around, and men of the same or younger age tend to choose younger women. For example, in the UK there are 295,000 widows, but only 65,000 widowers, over the age of 60.

MARRIAGE

The map shows the legal age of heterosexual marriage for women or, in many cases, girls. In all countries the age at which females are permitted to marry is the same as or earlier than that for males; nowhere is it at a later age. The youngest age at which a man can marry is at 14, in Chile and Paraguay. The highest permitted age is in China, where a man has to be 22 years of age before he can marry.

The law is widely disregarded in some countries, as shown by the *average* age of marriage appearing lower than the stated minimum legal age for women in several countries in Africa, Asia, and Latin America.

The global average age of marriage for girls is 22 years old; the country with the youngest average is Mali, at 16.4 years, and the country with the oldest is Sweden at 27.8 years.

Most studies show that good sex is important to a marriage, but in countries that have researched the factors for a happy marriage sex does not feature in the top five categories.

The piecharts "Married People have More Sex" show that, overall, married couples in the USA have more sex than the non-married. Additional data show that only 15 percent of married men and women seldom or never have sex, compared with about half of single men and women.

ADULTERY

Adultery, like fidelity, is universal, and recorded throughout history among both men and women. During the next 12-month period, five million people in the UK will be affected by infidelity. Attitudes towards adultery change. For example, the view of 50 percent of students in modern Shanghai that extra-marital sex is acceptable is considerably different from their parents' more conservative views.

Infidelity starts early. In the Durex 1999 survey of 14 countries around the world, 34 percent of sexually-active young people between 16 and 21 years of age (40 percent of men, 28 percent of women) said they had experienced a sexual relationship with more than one person at a time. Young Thai men are the most likely to have been unfaithful to a sexual partner (52 percent), probably reflecting the accessibility of Thailand's commercial sex industry. Other unfaithful nations include the USA, where 43 percent of young people have been unfaithful, Greece and the Czech Republic (both 38 percent).

Adultery is usually one of the main reasons for divorce; private-eye investigation agencies cite extra-marital affairs as top of their workload. At a personal level, it almost always causes emotional hurt.

Men react more strongly than women to the infidelity of their partners, as they want to bring up their own children. Female unfaithfulness puts this at risk (see **The Sex Drive** pp 12–13).

The line between chatting and cheating in cyberspace is invisible. Psychologists believe that cyber-flirting can be a dangerous business, and the legal status of betrayal of "online affairs" is yet to be resolved. There are many web sites offering advice about infidelity: how to spot it, how to recover from it, and whom to ask about it.

The reasons are unclear why, within our species, some men and women enjoy lifelong monogamy and others are promiscuous. It may be due to social constraints, practical opportunities, religious beliefs, or even to genetics. In 1998, researchers in the USA discovered a gene that may affect the extent to which people seek out different social partners. There are some places where adultery is institutionalized. In Germany, for example, there are 100 "couples-only" group sex clubs, where sex with strangers is increasing by 15 percent per year.

The map shows that four countries maintain the death penalty for adultery, although there have been no recent executions unless other crimes were involved. In Iran the laws are different for men and women. More often, it is the family who kill women suspected of adultery. In some countries of the Middle East and Latin America husbands are often exonerated from killing an unfaithful, disobedient or willful wife on the grounds of "honor."

Donating sperm for artificial insemination does not constitute legal adultery, even though the purpose is to impregnate another.

A chemical has been invented in Japan which, when sprayed on men's underwear, causes semen to glow bright green for up to a week, identifying a possibly straying husband.

DIVORCE

Marriage researchers in the USA believe it is possible to predict within three minutes whether a newly married couple is likely to divorce within the next six years.

Divorce rates vary hugely around the world. The lowest rate is in Afghanistan, where divorce is virtually unknown, followed by Spain, India, Lebanon, Syria, Iran. and Ecuador. The highest is in Hungary, followed by the USA and the Central African Republic. There are different grounds for divorce for men and for women in more than 30 Islamic, Asian and some African countries.

When the US Bureau of the Census reported 2.4 million marriages and 1.2 million divorces in one year, someone erroneously calculated, without taking into consideration the 54 million marriages already in existence, that half of all marriages fail. In fact, only about 2 percent of existing USA marriages break up in any single year.

Sex and violence are common grounds for divorce. In the UK adultery is the grounds in 23 percent of divorces granted to wives. In Shanghai, China, adultery is the reason cited in more than 50 percent of divorces.

Divorced people have less sex, more sex problems, more cancer, heart disease, and strokes, and live a shorter life than married or cohabiting couples.

Part Three REPRODUCTION

CONTRACEPTION

Up until the end of the nineteenth century, it was the norm for married women to carry on bearing children throughout their fertile years, the likelihood being that only a few of the babies would survive infancy and childhood to reach adulthood. Improvements in living conditions and advances in medical science resulted in dramatic falls in infant mortality rates during the twentieth century and led to couples wanting to reduce the number of births. The use of contraception has consequently increased in all countries of the world, in spite of continuing opposition from the Catholic Church, from community groups opposed to contraception being available to teenagers, and from some governments. Japan was forced to lift its ban on the contraceptive pill in 1999 after Japanese women protested that Viagra, in contrast, became immediately available for men with impotence. The Chinese government has shown a strong commitment to reducing family size: in the 1960s girls were encouraged to delay marriage and sex, and in the 1970s the "later-longer-fewer" campaign was introduced. Half the world's vasectomies are carried out in China.

Millions of fertile couples worldwide either cannot or do not use contraception even when it is freely available. For example, 1 in 10 sexually-active girls in the UK uses no contraception. The consequences are shown in the barchart "Teenage Abortions" (see p 43).

None of the varied methods of contraception is perfect – they are either cumbersome to use (such as the female condom), require taking pharmaceutical drugs (such as the Pill), or having a surgical procedure (such as insertion of IUCD or sterilization). The bar chart "Effectiveness of Contraceptive Methods" compares the reliability of various methods.

Three times as many women as men are sterilized, in spite of the fact that a vasectomy is a much easier operation. Women in rich countries are ten times more likely to request reversal than women in poor countries. Up until the 1970s, girls deemed socially or mentally inferior were sterilized in several industrialized countries. Concerns have been raised recently in some countries about people being "persuaded" to have a sterilization without them understanding the full implications.

The lowest average number of births in a woman's lifetime (under two births) is found mostly in the rich countries and in China; the highest (over six births) is mostly in Africa and the Middle East. Globally, about 50 percent of conceptions are unplanned, and about 25 percent are definitely unwanted.

About 600,000 women die each year in pregnancy or childbirth, or 1,600 every day. While in Europe the risk is one maternal death in 1,400 births, in Asia it is one in 65, and in Africa, one in 16. Family planning not only prevents births, it also saves the lives of women.

In the mid-1990s girls aged 15–19 gave birth to 17 million babies. That number is expected to drop to 16 million but not until 2025. Pregnancy and childbirth in adolescence pose higher risks for both mother and child.

Of the 41,700 children born each year in the UK to mothers aged 15–19, 87 percent are born outside marriage, the highest level of unmarried teenage motherhood in the world. That compares with 78 percent in France, 62 percent in the USA, 57 percent in Germany, and 10 percent in Japan. The rates of unplanned teenage pregnancies are also high in poor countries.

INFERTILITY

Infertility affects on average 8–12 percent of couples worldwide. Some couples are infertile from the start (known as primary infertility), whereas others become infertile after having a child (secondary infertility). Sometimes the cause is never found, and research is examining possible genetic, environmental and lifestyle factors.

Infertility in women increases with age. In addition to the causes of infertility shown on the map, causes of male infertility include: deficiencies in sperm production, blockage of the conducting system, antibodies against sperm, injuries to the testicles, hormone problems, poor descent of one or both testicles, or the presence of a varicocele.

Infertility has no effect upon sex drive or sexual performance, except through any stress brought about by pressure to conceive. Impotence from various causes may cause infertility because sperm, which may be perfectly normal, cannot reach the ovum.

There are wide variations in sperm count around the world, even within the same country – the range in the USA is from 48-134 million sperm per milliliter in apparently healthy males. There is ongoing controversy as to whether average sperm counts are falling, but nowhere do they appear to be rising.

CLONING

Until recently, scientists had believed that once adult cells had differentiated, to become skin or eye for example, their DNA would no longer be able to form a complete organism. This is now known to be not true and there is technically nothing to stop scientists from growing a full human being from such tissue in the future – only ethical considerations are likely to hold them back.

Currently, full human cloning is not legally practiced in any country. On the contrary, several countries have set legislation or guidelines to ban human cloning. More research needs to be done before it becomes safe or practical, and the process faces formidable medical, legal, and ethical hurdles. Also, cloning does not achieve the normal biological goal of passing on a shared genetic message as does the usual method of sexual reproduction.

A cloned individual will not be identical to the person from whom he or she is cloned. They may have the same appearance as the donor, but not necessarily the same nature, mental ability, character, or capacity of achievement. Replication is very different from resurrection. Identical twins are nature's clones, but frequently act in dissimilar ways and have separate conscious individualities. Upbringing is also a contributing factor in character formation, so that the human clone of a cruel dictator might turn out to be a philanthropist.

There are many potential problems, including that of finding a supply of surrogate mothers whose wombs would nurture the clones, until such time as scientists are able to grow human fetuses in the laboratory. Social complexities arising from cloning include that of producing identical twins of different ages, the aroused expectations of parents and the consequences for both parents and child if that child fails to live up to expectations, the child's right to know its originator and vice versa, resentment by a child at being genetically programmed, confusion about family relationships, and violation of the security of human genetic material.

While human cloning is inevitable, the critical task is to make sure, as with all new scientific procedures, that it is medically safe and ethically performed.

Part Four SEXUAL HEALTH

SEX EDUCATION

Most teenage years are typified by embarrassment, ignorance and confusion about sex which, in some cases, may continue into adulthood. Even without any sexual contact, young people may believe they have sexually-transmitted infections (STIs) and girls may fear they are pregnant; boys may be alarmed at their first nocturnal emission. The Samaritans' organization was founded in the UK after a young girl committed suicide when her first menstruation appeared, mistakenly thinking she had some serious disease. Homosexuals and lesbians face particular uncertainties during the teenage years, and rarely feel able to discuss their questions with parents, teachers or friends. Opposition to sex education in schools has sometimes been bitter, the issue having been taken to the courts in the USA. This has resulted in some self-censorship, with US teachers omitting discussion with their students of values, choices or decision-making, sexual pleasure, gay and lesbian issues, abortion and contraception.

Hundreds of studies have shown that sex education does not lead to earlier or increased sexual activity, as shown in the diagram "Going down/Going up." The only exception is programs that teach complete abstinence as the only option (rather than as one of a range of options).

The UN Convention on the Rights of the Child advocates rights to information, but even at its best, sex education rarely promotes the view that sexuality is a beautiful, natural component of life, or explains how to enhance and enjoy diverse sexual practices. Effectiveness of sex education is judged on adolescent pregnancy, abortion and STI rates, not on whether the young grow up to have happy sex lives.

Sex education is needed not only for youth but also for adults and health and other professionals. Sex education is becoming electronic. There are superb websites on the internet offering information, guidance and advice to people of all ages. The BBC World Service's "Sexwise" programs (see **Sex Education** pp 52–53) are broadcast in a wide variety of languages to millions of people around the world. The Robert Koch Institute in Berlin offers the most comprehensive website for health professionals and sexologists-in-training, with online courses in sexology, and links to sexology journals, reviews, institutes, archives, and other sexology websites.

SAFER SEX

If the six billion male condoms used each year were used properly, they would offer considerable protection against STIs. Condom failures usually occur because they are not used consistently and correctly, not because of manufacturing defects. About 0.5 percent of condoms break during vaginal intercourse and 3.6 percent during anal intercourse, but they still offer much greater protection than unprotected sex.

Female condoms, polyurethane bags inserted into the vagina before intercourse, were invented in the mid-1980s and offer women a barrier method they can control, with 95 percent effectiveness if used properly. Millions have been used, especially in Africa. They are popular, even if they squeak. Eighty-five percent of men like them because they do not need to use a rubber condom and also because polyurethane conducts heat more effectively than rubber so they feel nicer.

In the USA, one third of adults have changed their sex lives since knowing about the danger of HIV/AIDS: 29 percent use condoms more often (especially less-educated, single males), 26 percent practice monogamy

and 25 percent get to know their partners better before having sex. Yet studies in Europe and Africa show that only half of couples use condoms consistently where one partner is known to be HIV positive. Worldwide, increase in condom use has been most marked among commercial sex workers.

SEXUALLY-TRANSMITTED INFECTIONS

The earliest written reference to a sexually-transmitted infection is in the Old Testament of the Bible. In around 3,000 BC Moses killed many Midianite women captives for having gonorrhea. It was first described scientifically in 400 BC by the Greek physician Hippocrates.

STIs can sweep the world like wildfire. Columbus and his crew of 44 are commonly blamed for bringing syphilis to Europe from Haiti in 1493, which then spread all over the world within a few years. By early 1500 Europe was in the grip of an epidemic, and it reached China by 1505 and Japan a year later. In the twentieth century there was an enormous increase of STIs during the two world wars and the Vietnam war.

HIV started earlier than many people realize. Blood taken from patients with an undiagnosed fatal illness has been found, many years later, to contain HIV. The earliest-known example was from blood collected in 1959 from an adult male Bantu who lived in what is now the Democratic Republic of Congo. In Western countries the first documented example was a Norwegian sailor, probably infected in Cameroon in 1961. Since then, the virus has infected millions of people.

The number of STIs continues to grow. One in three sexually-active people in the USA has had a sexually transmitted infection by the age of 24.

While syphilis, gonorrhea, chlamydia, and trichomonas are STIs which can now be treated, viral STIs still cannot be eradicated. Seventy million people in the USA have an incurable STI viral infection such as herpes, human papillomavirus, hepatitis B, or HIV/AIDS. Many of the new STIs that will emerge in the twenty-first century will be initially incurable.

COUNSELING

The two most common sex problems in men are impotence and premature ejaculation. Impotence is the inability to achieve or maintain an erection; it may be present from birth, but more usually it develops after a period of normal erections, increases with age, and is caused by many factors such as tiredness, tobacco, alcohol, diabetes, and medication (for example, some treatments for high blood pressure). An estimated 50 million men in Europe and the USA have regular problems getting an erection. In Europe, one in ten men over the age of 18 experiences erection difficulties at least 50 percent of the time. Various forms of counseling, surgery, and pharmaceutical treatments can help. Premature ejaculation is when the man climaxes "too early," – a problem that responds well to therapy.

An unusual sex problem is "koro," whereby men in South East Asia, China and some parts of Africa experience terror in wrongly believing that their genitals are shrinking and disappearing inside their body.

The two most common sex problems in women are lack of interest in sex and not having an orgasm during sexual intercourse. Many societies still do not view either as a problem, and seem more concerned about the opposite – uncontrolled sexuality in women (see **Female Genital Excision** pp 74–75). Lack of sexual desire can be helped by counseling, using relaxation, and communication techniques, and the practicing of sensuous experiences. Most women can achieve an orgasm by masturbation, but some infrequently or never achieve orgasm during sexual intercourse; again this may respond to counseling.

Sexual problems in homosexuals are generally the same as those found in heterosexuals. Reported sex problems in men tend to increase with age but, with the exception of a decrease in vaginal lubrication post-menopause, women report fewer problems.

Part Five THE BUSINESS OF SEX

THE ECONOMICS OF SEX

Every topic in this atlas has either some economic debit or some financial gain to the individual or the state. Sometimes there is both gain and loss at the same time – to different people involved or affected.

Costs include medical and health costs and the costs of contraception; salaries or, on the other hand, loss of earnings; administering a justice system (e.g. for weddings, divorces, sex crimes); the costs of medical, legal and sociological research, journals and libraries; the costs of weddings, broken marriages, divorces and child sex abuse; and costs of counseling, pornography, prostitution, sex tourism and cosmetic surgery.

Who gains? A great many people – who work in all these fields, especially the organizers of the sex trade; purveyors of pornography (including film crews); sex tour operators; the film industry; writers of romantic novels; even doctors, lawyers and priests all benefit.

Measuring the overall global, even national, costs of sex in exact financial terms has never been attempted. The direct costs (e.g. of contraception, STIs) are difficult to measure, and it is even harder to quantify indirect but real costs (e.g. the cost to the state of supporting broken families). Above all, it is impossible to put a financial value on the joy and happiness sex can bring.

PORNOGRAPHY

Primary users of pornography are teenage boys and young men. It is not surprising that many turn to pornography for information on sex, as only 12 percent of young people find out about sex from their parents and 18 percent from school (see **Sex Education** pp 52–53). They are left to pick up knowledge from sexual partners and friends, or from sex magazines and electronic sources, which often contain violent and degrading images.

Many attempts have been made to protect children from sexually-explicit materials, by film ratings, legislation, and blocking internet sites. Such attempts are generally futile, so rather than attempting to censor pornography, one simple and less invasive policy solution would be to implement good sex education. Parents need to answer a simple question: "Where do you want your child to find out about sex? From sex education or from pornography?"

There is heated debate over the effects of pornography among leaders, feminists, parents, religious leaders, and the community in general. For example, the liberalization of pornography laws in the USA, UK, Australia, and the Scandinavian countries has been accompanied by a rise in the rates of reported rapes. But the rates of all violent crimes have increased and more women report rape, making it difficult to draw firm conclusions about the social effect of pornography.

Few studies differentiate between erotica, soft and hard porn, or take into account baseline norms. It is one thing to say that x percent of rapists read pornography before commiting a rape, but that statistic is meaningless unless it is known how many non-rapists read the same kind of porn. Further studies are needed to assess the effect of the various types of pornography.

Censorship laws are in a muddle all over the world – full of imprecise terminology as "offending public decency," or relying on "the notion of social harm, not necessarily the explictness of the sexual content." Different states in the USA have tried to censor things that would be "offensive by contemporary community standards" but are struggling to decide if an "average community member" is the same as "a reasonable community member." Some countries have tried to make a distinction between a woman naked from the waist up walking along the street either "in a provocative manner" or walking along "as a man would walk." In some countries action to ban offensive material is "complaint-driven," and in general, law and practice may be very different. In one South Asian country, a petrol station advertisement showing a female robot was banned as "it was not wearing clothes."

In general, the rich countries are more liberal than poor countries; Western nations more than Eastern nations. Currently, there is a global move towards liberalization, but as, historically, societies have oscillated, we may become more prudish in future.

PROSTITUTION

In 1949 the United Nations adopted a resolution in favor of decriminalizing prostitution, but many countries have still not ratified this resolution.

In a few countries, brothels are registered and prostitutes are licensed, with health checks and legal protection. In practice this can lead to taxes being imposed on prostitutes, restrictions on the areas in which they can work, corrupt practices surrounding their licensing and registration, and the imposition of punitive quarantine.

Although some prostitutes say they enjoy their job and the quick money it provides, more often than not they are children, victims of poverty, drug addicts, controlled by pimps, and have little or no job recognition, legal protection or access to adequate health care. Prostitutes' rights organizations are now fighting for better working conditions for their members.

SEX TOURISM

There are 700 million international tourist arrivals a year – a figure likely to increase to 967 million by 2010. International tourism has already become the top item in world exports and the biggest employer in the world. Every sixth job is dependent on, or related to, travel and tourism. Tourists and business travelers bring money into struggling economies that increasingly rely on tourism as their primary industry, including a local acceptance, or even promotion, of sex with children.

There are an increasing number of tourists who leave ethics and inhibitions at home and who travel specifically in search of sexual contact, in particular with children. Most international sex tourists are heterosexual men, although others also travel overseas in search of sex.

The travel industry has been slow to respond to this issue, and countries may fear clamping down on sex tourism may lead to a drop in foreign currency.

Several countries have enacted legislation to allow prosecution of their own citizens who abuse children overseas, such as Australia, Austria, Belgium, Canada, Denmark, France, Germany, Iceland, Ireland, Italy, Japan, New Zealand, Norway, Sweden, Switzerland, the UK, and the USA.

Part Six SEXUAL RITES

RELIGION

Many current controversial issues, such as homosexuality and abortion, are not specifically covered in the early doctrines of religions. When sacred readings deal specifically with sex matters, they sometimes do so in a contradictory manner. Therefore, some religious commentators believe it valid to extrapolate views on sexual behavior from their religion's general ethical teachings. For example: to treat others as one would wish to be treated; to refrain from exploiting, dominating, manipulating, being violent or abusive, and harming others, above all, children.

Religion continues to have a profound influence on many sexual matters, from contraception to divorce. The Children of God use sex for recruitment. In India and parts of Africa, some girls under six years must become the priest's "wife," in atonement for the family's past sins or to ensure their parents have a son. In 2000, 20,000 members of the Unification Church (Moonies) were married in Seoul's Olympic stadium. Many of the brides and grooms had never met before; some didn't even speak the same language. In the UK in 1995 the Church of England denied a homosexual the right to be godfather to his sister's son. In Brazil in 1996 a Catholic Bishop refused to marry a paraplegic man, because he would not be able to have sex and father children.

Despite homophobic attitudes from many religions, about two thirds of homosexual, bisexual and transgender religious youth questioned in the USA agreed with the statement: "I have no doubt that God loves me just as I am."

FEMALE GENITAL EXCISION

About 140 million women now living have undergone genital excision, with another two million being added to this total each year. The historical roots of FGE are obscure; it is thought to have originated in Egypt 2,000 years ago, preceding Christianity and Islam. Although practiced by some Christians such as the Russian Skoptozy sect, it is mostly performed in Islamic countries and in some areas in Africa. Yet the Prophet Mohammed never ordained or even favored FGE, and did not have it performed on his four daughters. FGE is not mentioned in the Koran, and it is not practiced in some devoutly Muslim countries, such as Iran, Iraq, Jordan, Libya or in Saudi Arabia.

In 1997 the United Nations called for an end to the practice.

CIRCUMCISION

The majority of men in the world, almost 80 percent, are not circumcised. Most of the 13 million circumcisions performed each year are done for religious or ritual reasons. The USA is the only medically advanced nation that still circumcises the majority of its male newborns for non-religious reasons.

Ritualistic circumcision has been carried out in West Africa for over 5,000 years, and in the Middle East for at least 3,000 years. Written documentation of circumcision first appears in the Bible. It surfaced as part of medical culture in North America and Europe only from the late nineteenth century for reasons that initially included "stopping masturbation," preventing or curing alcoholism, epilepsy, asthma, hernia, gout, rheumatism, curvature of the spine and headaches, then later for hygiene or to prevent penile and cervical cancer, urinary tract infections and STIs. Medical beliefs began to change around 1950 and it is now rarely done for medical reasons.

The complication rate is somewhere between one and ten percent. Even under the best surgical conditions, the death rate is 1 in 500,000 and in poor conditions may be as high as 1 in 24,000. The effects of pain on the newborn, and adverse sexual or psychological effects manifesting later in life, are mostly unknown.

Part Seven SEX CRIMES

SEXUAL HARASSMENT

In the animal world it is usually the male who makes the advances to the female, and who may receive initial rejection before final acceptance. Males also seek younger females, and females seek mates of higher status than themselves, so likewise in humans, relationships between professors and their students or managers and their employees are to be expected. In the

USA, at the beginning of the twenty-first century, 38 percent of office advances result in longterm relationships, but 9 percent end in formal harassment proceedings. At what stage advances become inappropriate, or office banter becomes offensive, can sometimes be difficult to define in law, but the key word is "unwanted."

The recipient may find it difficult to repel unwanted sexual advances if they are from someone with power over them, especially if their career and livelihood are at stake. Until relatively recently the victim of harassment at work had little redress in law, but that is beginning to change in a few countries.

In the USA, it is estimated that about one in six victims of sexual harassment are men, but only a small minority make formal complaints. Sexual harassment between people of the same gender is less common.

The word "stalking" comes from the vocabulary of hunting and implies a degree of stealth. In the twenty-first century, however, most stalkers do so visibly, arrogantly, and in full view of their prey. It is relatively uncommon for a women to stalk a man, but it is no less disturbing for the male victim.

The legal position on stalking varies from country to country, but in most countries stalking is defined as conduct that places a person in fear for their safety.

In the USA one in 12 women and one in 45 men have been stalked at some time in their life. Research shows six common stalker profiles: the batterer (most likely to kill); the pervert (takes sexual delight in torment); the jilted lover; the delusional stalker (after a celebrity); the psychotic stalker (believes he has been jilted by a stranger); and the narcissistic stalker.

Cyber-stalkers leave improper and harassing messages on message boards, chat rooms, discussion forums, and threatening or obscene email. Some US states have included cyber-stalking in their harassment legislation.

SEXUAL VIOLENCE

Sexual violence is based on issues of power, control, victimization and denial. It causes fear, pain, injury, sexually-transmitted infections, pregnancy, and physical and psychological scars in the victims. It happens in every class, culture, race, religion, and gender.

Rape is not a crime of passion, but a crime of violence, domination, humiliation and violation, by the stronger of the weaker. Asking a rape victim about her past behavior is as relevant as asking a robbery victim if he is a spendthrift. The issue is consent.

One in five US women is estimated to have been a victim of "date rape" by an acquaintance. Date rape is more likely to occur when either partner has been exposed to family violence. The risk is higher for girls who had their first date and/or sex at a young age. The date rape may be precipitated by relationship problems, alcohol and drug use, jealousy, who paid the expenses, who drove, the location, the misinterpretation of friendly cues as sexual invitations, or the assumption that sex is a reward for spending money on a girl or woman.

Elderly women over child-bearing age are raped, and homosexual rape occurs in prisons, discrediting the theory that rape is somehow a natural and biological product of man's evolutionary need to reproduce.

Pedophilia is sexual activity with pre-pubertal children. Two-thirds of molested victims are girls, usually aged between 8 and 11 years. To meet the diagnostic criteria, a pedophile must be at least 16 years old and at least five years older than the victim. According to Interpol, there are 30,000 pedophile groups in Europe alone, many linked through Internet. Most pedophiles are men, heterosexual and are often married with their own children. Eighty percent have a history of being sexually abuse themselves in childhood.

Some countries publish a sex offenders' index, but this distorts the true picture, as most sex abuse of children is committed not by strangers, but by people known to the child, such as family members, neighbors, family friends, baby-sitters, doctors, clergy, therapists, teachers and staff in children's homes. Abuse tends to take place over a long period of time.

Recently, some adults in industrialized countries have come to believe, under therapy, that they now remember previously-repressed memories of incest and sexual abuse during childhood. While some memories are accurate, others may represent a "False Memory Syndrome." Such recovered memories, true or false, are a tiny minority out of the global widespread sexual abuse of children. Most victims of sexual abuse remember it only too well.

Part Eight EVOLUTIONS

THE FUTURE OF SEX

Sex will not die out. People enjoy it too much. But it will change. Sex will become increasingly separated from reproduction, and parents, teachers, governments, and the legal, religious, medical, health, sociology, sexology and other professions will have to adjust to new sexual realities. The immediate future promises an era of more open attitudes and sexual practices.

This is nothing new. History has shown repeated cycles of liberalism and conservatism towards sex. But, for the first time, new technology will introduce undreamt of possibilities in the sexual arena. World trade in recreational sex industries will increase exponentially as these new technological developments become available. The strength of personal and family relationships will be strongly tested by these new possibilities. The ultimate effects are unclear.

REFERENCES

12-13 THE SEX DRIVE

Richard Dawkins, *The Selfish Gene*, Oxford University Press, Oxford, 1990; Oxford University Press, New York, 1989.

Matt Ridley, *The Red Queen: Sex and the Evolution of Human Nature*, Penguin, London, 1993.

William D. Hamilton, Public Understanding of Science: Evolution of Sex, University of Oxford web page:
<www.info.ox.ac/depts/zoology/brochure/evol.htm″sex>

Biodiversity: System Greater Than Sum of Its Parts
<www.acnatsci.org/erd/ea/biodiv45.html>

Anne Case, I-Fen Lin, Sara McLanahan, "How Hungry is the Selfish Gene?" NBER (National Bureau of Economic Research) Working Paper No. W7401, October 1999.

Part One SEXUALITY

18-19 FIRST ENCOUNTERS

FIRST SEX
Demographic and Health Surveys and Knowledge, Attitudes, Beliefs and Practices Surveys. (Published annually by DHS.)

Michel Hubert, Nathalie Bajos, Theo Sandfort, eds., *Sexual Behaviour and HIV/AIDS in Europe.* Institute of Education, University of London. UCL Press, 1998.

UNAIDS, 1998

Into A New World: Young Women's Sexual and Reproductive Lives. The Alan Guttmacher Institute, 1998: Table 3a, p 19.

SEXUAL TRENDS
Youth Risk Behavior Survey, USA 1998. Reported by Barbara Vobejda,"Steep Drop in Youngsters' Sexual Activity," *Washington Post*, in *The Guardian Weekly*, September 1998, p 13.

SEXUAL EXPERIENCES
Adolescents and their sexuality, Switzerland. Institut universitaire de medecine sociale et preventive, Lausanne, 1997

SEXUAL STAGES
E. Brugman *et al Jeugd en seks (Youth and Sex).* Witgeverij, SWP, 1995: Figure 4.1.

STARTING YOUNGER
Durex Global Sex Survey 1996, p6. Durex Condoms from London International Group plc.

VIRGINS
Durex Global Sex Survey 1997, p3. Durex Condoms from London International Group plc.

COMMENTARY ON THE MAPS
Amelia Gentleman,"Britain top for single teenage mothers," (International Planned Parenthood report) in *Guardian Weekly*, May 24, 1998, p11.

Singh and Wulf, The Alan Guttmacher Institute, "The percent of women 20–24 who had any sexual relationship before their 20th birthday by number of years of schooling, 1989," reported in *UNICEF, Adolescent health and development in Latin America and the Caribbean.*

20-21 SEXUAL PRACTICES

SEXUAL INTERCOURSE
*Durex Global Sex Surveys 1996, 199*8 Durex Condoms from London International Group plc

Brazil: "Rio top of league for sex," *Eastern Express*, April 9, 1996.

France: "French get bored with endless sex," *South China Morning Post*, August 1, 1997, p 23.

India: John Zubrzycki in New Delhi, "Sedate sex life customs shed after wedding night," *South China Morning Post*, September 6, 1996, p 18.

USA (top): Marie Dewitt, *The Harlequin Romance Report 1999*, Harlequin Enterprises Limited and Torstar, <www.romance.net>.

USA (bottom): Barbara Vobejda,"Things That Make You Feel Sexy," in *Washington Post/International,* U.S., reported in *Guardian Weekly,* 25 Jan 1998, p 15

NUMBER OF SEX PARTNERS
SURVEY.NET Poll Results – Sex Survey #1 Inter Commerce Corporation Home page URL (http://www.survey.net)

BONDAGE
K.E. Ernulf, S.M. Innala, "Sexual bondage: a review and unobtrusive investigation," Department of Psychology, Goteborg University, Sweden. *Archive Sexual Behavior* December 1995; 24(6), pp 631–54.

ORGASMS
Robert T Michael, John H Gagnon, Edward O Laumann, Gina Kolata, "Sex in America: A definitive survey," *National Health and Social Life Survey,* NHSLS 1992. Little, Brown and Co., 1994.

WHATEVER TURNS YOU ON
Michael *op cit*

SEXUAL ORIENTATION
SURVEY.NET *op cit*

THINKING ABOUT SEX
Michael *op cit*

COMMENTARY ON THE MAPS
Michael *op cit*

Stephanie A. Sanders, June Machover Reinisch, "Would You Say You "Had Sex" If...?" January 20, 1999. *Journal of the American Medical Association* 1999; 281. pp 275–77

AFP in London, "Health: Life's three year feast," in *South China Morning Post*, May 8, 1998, p 12.

"Fertility problems in the middle years," *International Planned Parenthood Federation*, 1/2, 1979.

22-23 HOMOSEXUALITY

LEGAL STATUS
World Legal Survey, International Lesbian and Gay Association, 2000. <www.ilga.org>

Amnesty International <www.amnesty.org>

Interpride, 1999 <www.interpride.org>

Same sex activity: "There's nowt so queer as animals," *Sunday Times*, June 27, 1999, p 13 (Book Review: *Biological Exuberance: Animal homosexuality and natural diversity*, by Bruce Bagemihi)

"Between 3% and 4% ...", Eli Coleman, Workshop on Psychotherapy for Gay Men and Lesbians, 14th World Congress of Sexology, Hong Kong; August 23-27, 1999.

Thailand: A.S. London *et al* "Socio-demographic correlates, HIV/AIDS-related cofactors, and measures of same-sex sexual behaviour among northern Thai male soldiers," *Health Transit Review*, April 1997, 7(1), pp 33-60.

General: Gill Dunne, London School of Economics, quoted in "Gay men make better fathers, claims research," *Scotland on Sunday,* January 9, 2000, p 1.

GAY PRIDE MARCH
"Loud and proud at 25," *The Observer,* in *The Guardian Weekly* for week ending July 13, 1997, p 8.

SAME SEX PARTNERS
Tom W. Smith, "American Sexual Behavior: Trends, Socio-Demographic Differences, and Risk Behavior," National Opinion Research Center, University of Chicago, General Social Survey (GSS) Topical Report No. 25, Table 8B, December, 1994.

COMMENTARY ON THE MAPS
F. L. Whitam, C. Daskalos, C. G. Sobolewski, P. Padilla,"The emergence of lesbian sexuality and identity cross-culturally: Brazil, Peru, the Philippines, and the United States," *Archive Sexual Behavior,* February 1998, 27(1), pp 31-56.

R. Blanchard, A. F. Bogaert, "Biodemographic comparisons of homosexual and heterosexual men in the Kinsey Interview Data," *Archive of Sexual Behavior*, December 1996, 25(6), pp 551-79.

World Legal Survey, The International Lesbian and Gay Association (ILGA), 2000, <www.ilga.org>

Jones, D.A., "Discrimination against same-sex couples in hotel reservation policies," *Journal of Homosexuality* 1996, 31 (1-2), pp 153-59.

The National Coalition for Gay, Lesbian, Bisexual and Transgender Youth and Oasis Magazine, !OutProud!/Oasis Internet Survey of Queer and Questioning Youth, March 1998. <www.oasismag.com/survey/97/>

24-25 TRANSGENDER

GENDER REASSIGNMENT
Press for Change, International Bill of Gender Rights, 1995 <www.pfc.org.uk/gendrpol/gdrights.htm>

Gender legislation, Gender Talk, 1999

Liberty, 21 Tabard Street, London SE1 4LA: liberty@gn.apc.org

The International Lesbian and Gay Association, World Legal Survey, 2000. <www.ilga.org>

Robert T. Franceour, *The International Encyclopedia of Sexuality.* Continuum, New York, 1999.

Estimated numbers worldwide: Dr. Anne Fausto-Sterling, Professor of Medical Science, Brown University, USA, reported in Intersex Society of North America,

Louis Gooren, Vrije Univ, Netherlands, in "Psychological and hormonal treatment of gender dysmorphia" workshop at the 14th World Congress of Sexology, Hong Kong; 1999.

A NEW IDENTITY
Liberty, *op cit*

COMMENTARY ON THE MAPS
Fausto-Sterling *op cit*

R. Green, "Sexual Identity Of 37 Children Raised By Homosexual Or Transsexual Parents," *American Journal of Psychiatry* 1978, 135, 6, pp 692-97.

Gill Dunne, London School of Economics, quoted in "Gay men make better fathers, claims research," *Scotland on Sunday*, January 9, 2000, p 1.

Part Two MATING

28-29 SEX APPEAL

Waist-hip ratio: D. Singh, "Adaptive significance of female physical attractiveness: role of waist to hip ratio." *Journal Personal Social Psychology* 1993; 65, pp 293, 307

J. Connolly, L. Mealey & V. Slaughter (in press) "Development of Preference for Body Shapes," *Perspectives in Human Biology.*

Japan (top): Robbie Swinnerton, *Sunday Morning Post*, May 31, 1998 p 6.

Japan (bottom): Denise Campbell "Asian women fall prey to the 'thin is beautiful' culture" *Asian Medical News*, July 1998, p 5.

UK (top): Libby Brooks *Guardian* September 23, 1997

UK (bottom): "The Truth about Women: Love and Sex", Meridian Broadcasting, May 11, 1999

USA: Jonathan Freedland, "Looks don't matter says 'ugly' American," *The Observer* in *South China Morning Post*, June 14, 1996, p 19

THE SUCCESS OF SYMMETRY
Randy Thornhill, University of New Mexico, reported by Tania Unsworth, "The symmetrical art of falling in lust," *Sunday Times Magazine*, in *South China Morning Post*, December 28, 1996, p R3.

SEXUAL SMELL
Ingelore Ebberfeld, *Botenstoffe der Liebe – ber das innige Verhältnis von Geruch und Sexualität,* Frankfurt/M.: Campus 1998, p 252.

COSMETIC SURGERY/THE COST OF SURGERY
1998 Plastic Surgery Procedural Statistics, National
Clearinghouse of Plastic Surgery Statistics, American Society of
Plastic and Reconstructive Surgeons (ASPRS) web site:
www.plasticsurgery.org

COMMENTARY ON THE MAPS
"Science briefing: Pretty boys preferred," *South China Morning
Post,* September 7, 1998, p 20.

"Pensions make the heart grow fonder," *Sunday Morning Post*,
February 23, 1997, p 16. (Research from British insurance
company Eagle Star)

Ian Pearson. *The Macmillan Atlas of the Future* Macmillan, New
York, 1998; *The Atlas of the Future*, Routledge, London, 1998.

30-31 DATING

SEX ON A DATE
WHO, 1999

UNAIDS, AIDS Epidemic Update: December 1999
<www.unaids.org>

International Planned Parenthood Federation (IPPF), 1990s.

POPLINE (Population Information Program, Center for
Communication Programs, Johns Hopkins University)

B. Traeen, I. L. Kvalem,"Sexual socialization and motives for
intercourse among Norwegian adolescents," *Archive Sexual
Behavior* June 1996 25(3), pp 289–302.

*Into A New World: Young Women's Sexual and Reproductive
Lives.* The Alan Guttmacher Institute, 1998: Table 3a, p 19.

Adolescents and their sexuality, Switzerland. Institut universitaire
de medecine sociale et preventive, Lausanne, 1997

Hong Kong: Naomi Lee, "Younger children drawn to sex," *South
China Morning Post*, May 30, 1997, p 3.

India: Paul Sachdev, "Sexual evolution or sexual revolution: a
study of attitudes and behaviors among university students in
Delhi, India" 14th World Congress of Sexology, Hong Kong;
23–27 August 1999, Abstract book p 108.

Thailand: Surasak Taneepanichskul, "Sexual behavior of Thai
male before marriage," Poster, 14th World Congress of Sexology.
Abstract book p 331.

USA (left and general): Marie Dewitt *The Harlequin Romance
Report 1999* <www.romance.net>

USA (right, top): Autumn Oswald, "Issues of Adolescent Dating:
When do Adolescents date?" *Social Changes*,
September 1, 1999

USA (right, bottom): V. I Rickert, C. M. Wiemann "Date rape
among adolescents and young adults," *Journal of Pediatric
Adolescent Gynecology*, 11(4) November 1998, pp 167–75

MAKING OUT
Adolescents and their sexuality, Switzerland. *op cit*

OFFICE DATING
Marie Dewitt, *op cit*

INTERNET DATING
Mike Perry, SURVEY.NET Poll Results – Sex Survey #1,
1995–1999 Inter Commerce Corporation, <www.survey.net>

WHERE PARTNERS FIRST MEET
Robert T Michael, John H Gagnon, Edward O Laumann, Gina
Kolata, "Sex in America: A definitive survey," National Health
and Social Life Survey, NHSLS 1992, Little, Brown and Co., 1994.

COMMENTARY ON THE MAPS
D. K. Wysocki, "Let your fingers do the talking: sex on an adult
chat-line," *Sexualities* 1(4), 1999, p 425

SURVEY.NET *op cit*

"Find me a find, catch me a catch," *Asia Magazine*,
October, 10-12, 1997.

Tim Phillips, "Online: Got a match?" *The Guardian*, February 13,
1997, p 4.

Alex Lo, "Money can't buy love," *South China Morning Post*,
May 5, 1997, p 5.

32-33 CHOOSE YOUR PARTNER

OLDER MEN, YOUNGER WOMEN
David M. Buss, "Sex differences in human mate preferences:
Evolutionary hypothesis tested in 37 cultures," *Behavioral and
Brain Sciences*, 1989, 12, pp 1–49.

China: Debbie Taylor, *Servile Marriage: a definition, a survey
and the start of a campaign for change,* Oxford, March 1993,
p 20.

Gambia: *Situation of Women and Children in Gambia*, UNICEF
1993.

QUALITIES SOUGHT IN A MATE
David M. Buss, "International preferences in selecting mates.
A study of 37 cultures", *Journal of Cross-Cultural Psychology*,
vol. 21, no. 1, March 1990, pp 5-47.

TRAFFIC IN MAIL ORDER BRIDES
Taylor *op cit* pp 36–37.

NOT JUST A PRETTY FACE
Douglas T. Kenrick and Richard C Keefe "Time to integrate
sociobiology and social psychology". *Behavioral and Brain
Sciences* (1989)12, pp 24–25.

COMMENTARY ON THE MAPS
Joji Sakurai, "Japanese typecast by blood," *South China Morning
Post*, December 12, 1997, p 25.

Ng Man Lun. *Hong Kong Medical Association Newsletter*,
June 1995, pp 29–30.

Robert Benewick and Stephanie Donald, *The State of China
Atlas*, Penguin, London and New York, 1999, p 12.

Tim Phillips, "Online: Got a match?" *The Guardian*, February 13,
1997, p 4.

34-35 MARRIAGE

Population Reports, Population Information Programme, Johns Hopkins University, December 1992, p 26.

The World's Youth 1994, "Average age at first marriage." Population Reference Bureau, The Center for Population Options.

LEGAL AGE OF MARRIAGE FOR WOMEN
International Planned Parenthood Federation (IPPF), 1996

International Womens Rights Action Watch, 1996
Joanne O'Brien and Martin Palmer, *The State of Religion Atlas*, Simon & Schuster, London and New York, 1993.

Canada: Personal communication, Ministry of Health, Canada, 1999

USA: Personal communication, Department of Health and Human Services, USA, 1999

India: John Zubrzycki, "Sedate sex life customs shed after wedding night" *South China Morning Post*, September 6, 1996, p 18.

China: AFP, "Sex imbalance sees females outnumbered 120–100," *South China Morning Post,* January 8, 1999, p 8.

MARRIED PEOPLE HAVE MORE SEX
James A. Davis and Tom W. Smith, *The General Social Survey. American Sexual Behavior: Trends, Socio-Demographic Differences, and Risk Behavior.* National Opinion Research Center (NORC), University of Chicago. GSS Topical Report No. 25, 1994, Table 8: p 116.

COMMENTARY ON THE MAPS
Population Reference Bureau, *op cit*

James A. Davis *op cit* Tables 8 and 10

36-37 ADULTERY

INFIDELITY
Durex Global Sex Survey 1998 Condoms from London International Group plc

WHO, 1990s

Jerry Adler, "Adultery: A New Furor Over and Old Sin" *Newsweek*, September 30, 1996, pp 36–44.

Philip Elmer-Dewitt, "Now for the truth about Americans and Sex." *Time Magazine* October 17, 1994, pp 52–58.

Amnesty International, 1999

FORGIVEN
E Suiero *et al.* "Comparison of sexual attitudes." Vigo's University (Ourense Campus), Spain. Poster, 14th World Congress of Sexology, Hong Kong; 23–27 August 1999. Abstract p 322.

DISCOVERY/CONFESSIONS AND SUSPICIONS/WHO IS THE LOVER?
Laisee, "Shock finding," *South China Morning Post*, Hong Kong. September 12, 1995: p B20

Harris Research Centre, reported on ITV London Weekend Television "Infidelity", March 12, 1999.

VIEWS ON ADULTERY in the USA
Jerry Adler, *op cit*

VIEWS ON ADULTERY in the UK
Kay Wellings, Anne Johnson, Jane Wadsworth, and Julia Field, *National Survey of Sexual Attitudes and Lifestyles*, UK, 1996

COMMENTARY ON THE MAPS
ITV London Weekend Television *op cit*

"A sexual revolution of sorts is sweeping Shanghai campuses," *Far East Economic Review*, September 26, 1996.

Durex Global Sex Survey 1999: A youth perspective, Durex Condoms from London International Group plc

"Phone taps and undercover films are all in a days work for a private eye," *Sunday Hong Kong Standard*, August 4, 1996, p 4.

Valerie Rice, "Your Cheatin' Heart," Ziff-Davis TV Inc. July 15, 1996.
Sunday Times in London, "Scientists unearth 'promiscuity' gene," reported in *South China Morning Post*, February 16, 1998, p 1

Denis Staunton, "Germany comes together," *The Observer*, in *Sunday Morning Post*, January 15, 1995, p 3.

Cecil Marie Cancel,"Honor Killings," About.com, August 18, 1999.

Sally Fisher, "Spray-can to unmask cheating partners," *South China Morning Post*, June 8, 1999, p 13.

38-39 DIVORCE

SEPARATED
U.S. Bureau of the Census, International Data Base. On Internet:

Australia: P. Jordan, Family Court of Australia, quoted in Sue Green, "Men find it hard to deal with divorce", *South China Morning Post*, December 10, 1996, p 24.

UK: *National Child Development Survey*, UK, 1995

Malaysia: Ian Stewart, "Women outraged by new polygamy law," *South China Morning Post*, October 22, 1996, p 19.

China: Bob Benewick and Stephanie Donald, *The State of China Atlas*, Penguin, London and New York, 1999, p 66.

MEN GET RICHER, WOMEN POORER
Linda Kozak, National Organization of Women, reported by Victoria McKee in "Real-life soap can clean out bank accounts," *South China Morning Post* June 27, 1989, p 20.

COMMENTARY ON THE MAPS
"Divorce predicted in minutes," University of Washington report quoted in *South China Morning Post*, October 6, 1999, p 11.

J. Allan Petersen, "Preaching Resources," *Better Families, Christianity Today*, Summer 1996 Vol. XVII, No.3, p 69. On <www.divorcereform.org>

Alex Bellos, "Slump blamed for record divorces," *Guardian Weekly*, September 3, 1995.

"Hooked on infidelity," *South China Morning Post*, October 9, 1996, p 10.

Emily Laurence Baker, "Cupid's role in a healthier life," *The Guardian*, in *South China Morning Post*, February 11, 1999, p 15.

Part Three REPRODUCTION

42-43 CONTRACEPTION

Institute of Medicine Report, USA, 1999, <www.nas.edu>

"The morning after," *The Economist*, August 2, 1996.

Reproductive health in the world: bare facts. Global reproductive health, WHO Biennial Report 1990-1991.

USE OF CONTRACEPTION
United Nations, Population Division, 1999, <www.un.org>

World Health Organization, 1999.

Shanti R Conly, Nada Chaya, Karen Helsing, *Contraceptive Choice: Worldwide Access to Family Planning*, Population Action International, 1997.

STERILIZATION
Population Reports: Voluntary Female Sterilization: Number One and Growing. November 1990. Population Information Program, Center for Communication Programs, The Johns Hopkins University School of Public Health, USA.

Population Reports: Vasectomy: New Opportunities. March 1992.

INCREASING ACCESS TO CONTRACEPTION WORLDWIDE
Shanti R Conly, Nada Chaya, Karen Helsing, "Contraceptive Choice: Worldwide Access to Family Planning," Population Action International, 1997.

TEENAGE ABORTIONS
Office of National Statistics, UK, reported in "UK eyes Dutch sex lessons," *The Observer*, February 21, 1999, p 12.

EFFECTIVENESS OF CONTRACEPTIVE METHODS
Population Reports, series J, Number 48, Dec 1998, p 26. Population Information Program, Center for Communication Programs, The Johns Hopkins University School of Public Health, USA.

COMMENTARY ON THE MAPS
Robert Benewick and Stephanie Donald, *The State of China Atlas*, Penguin, London and New York, 1999, p 106

"Chinese have half the world's vasectomies", *Asian Medical News*, December 1997, p 5.

Population Reports. op cit

David Fletcher, Health Correspondent, "More women are having sex without precautions," *Daily Telegraph*, September 20, 1996, p 7.

Daniel J Kevles, "Education and debate: Eugenics and human rights," *British Medical Journal*, August 14, 1999, 319, pp 435–38.

"Eugenics and the welfare state: sterilization policy in Denmark, Sweden, Norway, and Finland." in G. Broberg and N. Roll-Hansen, eds., Michigan State University Press, 1996.

H.D. Taubert , "Forced sterilization 1933–1945: an attempt at coming to terms with the past," [Article in German], Zentralbl Gynakol 1998, 120(1), pp 21–25.

H. M. Hanauske-Abel, "Not a slippery slope or sudden subversion: German medicine and national socialism in 1933," *British Medical Journal*, December 7, 1996, 313 (7070), pp 1453–63.

Emily Buchanan, "Playing God with people's lives," *The Guardian Weekly* Volume 156 issue 12 for week ending March 23, 1997, p 30

Nicole Bonnet in Lima, "Sterilisation drive alarms Peruvian women," *Le Monde/International*, in *Guardian Weekly*, volume 180, January 11, 1998, p 18.

Alex Bellos in Rio de Janeiro, "Indian women 'sterilised for votes' in Brazil," *The Guardian Weekly*, September 27, 1998, p 5.

Amnesty 1998 Press Release, "Amnesty joins in Condemning the Attacks against Peruvian Women's Rights Activist," New York, 1998.

Pam Belluck, New York Times in Chicago, "Sterilised addicts given cash: Controversial programme pays women $1,500 to lose their fertility," in *South China Morning Post*, July 7, 1999, p 12.

Roger Dean du Mars in Seoul, "Government 'covered up illegal sterilisation of retarded people,'" *South China Morning Post*, August 23, 1999, p 10.

44-45 PREGNANCY

"Reproductive health in the world: bare facts," Global reproductive health, WHO Biennial Report 1990-1991

GIVING BIRTH
World Demographic Data/Maps, US Bureau of the Census 1999

International Planned Parenthood Federation (IPPF).

TEEN BIRTHS
Population Action International, *Reproductive Risk: A worldwide assessment of women's sexual and maternal health,* 1995 report on progress towards world population stabilization.

FUTURE FAMILY SIZES
World Demographic Data/Maps, *op cit*

COMMENTARY ON THE MAPS
World Health Organization, *The World Health Report 1998 Life in the 21st century: A vision for all.* p 7

World Health Organization, *Fifty facts from The World Health Report 1998: Global health situation and trends 1955–2025.*

The Alan Guttmacher Institute, *Into A New World: Young Women's Sexual and Reproductive Lives,* 1998, Appendix Table 4, p 52.

46-47 INFERTILITY

World Health Organization, Division of Family Health, Programme on Maternal and Child Health and Family Planning, "Infertility: a tabulation of available data on prevalence of primary and secondary infertility," WHO/MCH/91.9.

Cigarettes: What the Warning Label Doesn't Tell You: The First Comprehensive Guide to the Health Consequences of Smoking, The American Council on Science and Health, New York, 1996.

INFERTILITY
Population Action International, *Reproductive Risk: A worldwide assessment of women's sexual and maternal health,* 1995

HEAT EXHAUSTION
R. J. Levine *et al* "Differences in the quality of semen in outdoor workers during summer and winter." Journal of Medicine, July 5, 1990; 323(1), pp 12-16.

CLOCK
A. Cagnacci *et al*, "Diurnal variation of semen quality in human males," *Human Reproduction* January 1999, 14(1), pp 106–09.

ALCOHOL IMPEDES PREGNANCY
Tina Kold Jensen *et al* "Does moderate alcohol consumption affect fertility? Follow-up study among couples planning first pregnancy," *British Medical Journal* August 22, 1998; 317, pp 505–10.

COMMENTARY ON THE MAPS
World Health Organization op cit

48-49 CLONING

CLONING LAW
IFFS Surveillance 98, *Fertility and Sterility*, 1999, vol 71, no 5, Supplement 2, p 288. Reprinted with permission from the American Society for Reproductive Medicine.

Human Genetics Advisory Commission (UK), "Cloning issues in reproduction, science and medicine," issued December 1998, <www.dti.gov.uk/hgac/>
Lebanon and Saudi Arabia: AFP in Riyadh, "Cleric urges death for clone scientists," *South China Morning Post*, March 14, 1997, p 22.

USA 1997: "Jesuit priest proclaims cloned human would have a different soul," *South China Morning Post*, February 26, 1997, Focus p 17.

USA 1997: Raelian religious movement: Gina Kolata and Philip Cohen, "Ethical dilemma in the lap of the gods," *South China Morning Post*, June 16, 1997, p 25.

France 1999: Judy Jones, "News: Cloning may cause health defects," *British Medical Journal* May 8, 1999, 318, p 1230.

FUTURE DEVELOPMENTS
Ian Pearson, *The Macmillan Atlas of the Future*, Macmillan, New York, 1998; Routledge, London, 1998.

PUBLIC OPINION
CNN Poll: "Most Americans say cloning is wrong," March 1, 1997, <www.cnn.com/TECH/9703/01/clone.poll/index.html>

COMMENTARY ON THE MAPS
Raanan Gillon, "Human reproductive cloning – a look at the arguments against it and a rejection of most of them," *Journal of the Royal Societyof Medicine*, 1999, 92, pp 3–12.

Part Four SEXUAL HEALTH

52-53 SEX EDUCATION

FINDING OUT – FROM AFAR
International Planned Parenthood Federation (IPPF) and the BBC World Service Education (BBC), "Sexwise," 1999. <www.bbc.co.uk/worldservice/sexwise

FINDING OUT – FROM CLOSE BY
Durex Global Sex Survey, 1999: A youth perspective. Durex Condoms from London International Group plc

Malaysia: "Sexual Ingnorance," South China Morning Post, October 19, 1999, p 13.

FIRST SEX EDUCATION
Durex Global Sex Survey, 1999: A youth perspective op cit fig.1.4.

GOING DOWN/GOING UP
L. S. Zabin, "School-linked reproductive health services: the Johns Hopkins Program," in: *Preventing adolescent pregnancy: model programs and evaluations*, ed. Brent C. Miller *et al* Sage Publications, 1992, pp 156–84.

KNOWLEDGE OF SEX
AFP in Manila, McCann Erickson, survey reported in "Sex a duty and rape a key worry, women tell study," *South China Morning Post*, September 8, 1998, p 10.

COMMENTARY ON THE MAPS
J.M. Paxman and R.J. Zuckerman, "Laws and policies affecting adolescent health," WHO, Geneva, 1987, pp 47–49, 53.

S. Ross and L.M. Kantor, "Trends in opposition to comprehensive sexuality education in public schools: 1994–95 school year," *Sex Information and Educational Council of the U.S.* [SIECUS], August–September 1995; 23(6), pp 9–15.

R. Stutsman, "Sex, lies, and Title XX," *ZPG Reporter*, April 1992, 24(2), p 3.

D. W. Haffner, "Sex education 2000: a call to action," *Sex Information and Educational Council of the U.S.* [SIECUS], New York, March 1990.

K. Mahler, "Condom availability in the schools: lessons from the courtroom," *Family Planning Perspectives*, March–April 1996, 28(2), pp 75–77.

Janet B. Hardy and Laurie Schwab Zabin, "Adolescent pregnancy in an urban environment: issues, programs and evaluation," in *The Self Center: program evaluation*, Urban Institute Press, Washington, D.C., 1991, pp 339–55.

S. Philliber and J. P. Allen, "Life options and community service: Teen Outreach Program." in *Preventing adolescent pregnancy: model programs and evaluations* edited by Brent C. Miller *et al*, Sage Publications, Newbury Park, CA, 1992, pp 139–55.

M. Eisen and G.L. Zellman, "A health beliefs field experiment: Teen Talk." in *Preventing adolescent pregnancy: model programs and evaluations* ed. Brent C. Miller *et al, op cit*

E.M. Mink, L. Mareth L, J. Russell, and M. Young, "Correlates of condom use among fraternity men," *Psychological Reports*, February 1991, 68(1), pp 255–58.

Robert Koch Institute, Berlin, <www.rki.ge/GESUND/ARCHIV/HOME.HTM>

Chinese language youth internet web site on love, relationships and sex. <dotlove.com>

54-55 SAFER SEX

CONDOMS
World Population Profile. US Bureau of the Census, 1999.

Population Reports, Population Information Center, The Johns Hopkins School of Public Health, USA, Sept 1990, p 5.

World Contraception Use, UN Dept for Economic and Social Information and Policy Analysis, Population Division, UN Dept for Economic and Social Information and Policy Analysis, United Nations, New York, NY, USA, 1994.

Durex Global Sex Survey, 1996 Durex Condoms from London International Group plc, p 17

RELATIONSHIP STATUS
Durex Global Sex Survey, 1996, op cit

BEING PREPARED
Durex Global Sex Survey, 1996, op cit

COMMENTARY ON THE MAPS
Joel R. Cooper, "Low odds, high risk," *The Medical Reporter*, April 9, 1996.

Johns Hopkins University, *Condom User Profiles*, April 1, 1996, pp 6-7.

Family Health International [FHI], "The female condom: frequently asked questions," NETWORK, September 1995, 16(1), pp 24-5.

Christina Stucky, "It's arrived and it's popular, even if it squeaks," *The Sunday Independent,* Cape Town, April 26, 1998, p 8.

K.H. Choi and J. A. Catania, "Changes in multiple sexual partnerships, HIV testing, and condom use among US heterosexuals 18 to 49 years of age, 1990 and 1992," *Journal of American Public Health Association*, April 1996, Vol 86, No 4, pp 554-55.

S. Allen *et al*, "Effect of serotesting with counselling on condom use and seroconversion among HIV discordant couples in Africa," *British Medical Journal* 1992, 304, pp 1605-09.

I. De Vincenzi, "A longitudinal study of human immunodeficiency virus transmission by heterosexual partners," *New England Journal of Medicine*, 1994; 331, pp 341-56.

56-57 SEXUALLY-TRANSMITTED INFECTIONS
AIDS
UNAIDS/WHO Report on the global HIV/AIDS epidemic, "Estimated number of people living with HIV/AIDS, end 1997," (adult rate) June 1998, pp 64-66.

Sub-Saharan Africa: UNAIDS Joint United Nations Program on HIV/AIDS, "AIDS epidemic update," December 1998, <www.unaids.org>

Cambodia: Joe Cochrane, "Troops face unseen enemy as HIV sweeps through ranks," *South China Morning Post*, March 31, 1999, p 10.

China: "Increase in sexual diseases," *South China Morning Post*, March 30, 1996, p 9.

Thailand: D. D. Celentano *et al* "HIV-1 infection among lower class commercial sex workers in Chiang Mai, Thailand," *AIDS*, April 1994;8(4), pp 533-37.

USA: Janice Hopkins Tanne, "News: US has epidemic of sexually transmitted disease," *British Medical Journal*, December 12, 1998; 317, p 1616.

ASPECTS OF LOVE
"An Overview of Selected Curable Sexually-Transmitted Diseases," Table 1: Estimated prevalence and annual incidence of curable STDs by region. WHO Initiative on HIV/AIDS and Sexually Transmitted Infections (HSI), 1999, <www.who.ch>

ONE-NIGHT STAND
"Chances of acquiring a STD after one episode of intercourse with infected person," STD Reference Centre of the South African Institute for Medical Research, June 1998.

WHO GETS AIDS?
Michael W Adler, "Sexual health – a Health of the Nation failure," *British Medical Journal*, June 14, 1997, no. 7096 vol. 314, pp 1743-47.

ANATOMY OF AN EPIDEMIC
UNAIDS Joint United Nations Program on HIV/AIDS, "AIDS epidemic update," December 1998, <http://www.unaids.org>.

COMMENTARY ON THE MAPS
Reuters, "Aids virus traced to 1930s cull of chimps," *South China Morning Post*, February 2, 2000, p 13.

"Early European AIDS," *New Scientist*, July 16, 1989, p 30.

Janice Hopkins Tanne, *op cit*

58-59 COUNSELING

SEXUAL PROBLEMS (USA)
Robert T Michael, John H Gagnon, Edward O Laumann, Gina Kolata, "Sex in America: A definitive survey," *National Health and Social Life Survey, NHSLS 1992*. Little, Brown and Co., 1994.

UK: "On the couch," *South China Morning Post*, April 6, 1993, p 7.
SUCCESSFUL COUNSELING
Peter McCarthy and Marj Thorburn, *Psychosexual Therapy at Relate: A report on cases processed between 1992–1994*. Relate Centre for Family Studies, University of Newcastle upon Tyne.

FAQs...
various internet sites

GIVING SEX ADVICE
"Doctors and Medical students giving advice in Latin America, 1989," Population Information Program, Center for Communication Programs, Johns Hopkins University.

SEXUAL SATISFACTION
Peter McCarthy *op cit*

SEXUAL PROBLEMS (INDIA)
K. K. Verma, B. K. Khaitan, and O. P. Singh, "The frequency of sexual dysfunctions in patients attending a sex therapy clinic in north India," *Archive Sexual Behavior*, June 1998, 27(3), pp 309-14.

COMMENTARY ON THE MAPS
Edward Helmore of *The Guardian* in New York, "Wait over for impotency pill," *South China Morning Post*, April 13, 1998, p 8.

"Hard facts," *The Guardian*, September 7, 1996.

A. N. Chowdhury, "Penile perception of Koro patients," *Acta Psychiatrica Scandanavica*, August 1989, 80(2), pp 183-86.

R. Durst, A. Teitelbaum, S. Cohen, P. Rosca-Rebaudengo, "Koro syndrome – clinical and cultural aspects," [Article in Hebrew], *Harefuah*, June 1, 1993, 124(11), pp 673-76, 740.

Part Five THE BUSINESS OF SEX

62-63 THE ECONOMICS OF SEX

THE COST OF SEX
Patrick Dixon, Director of Global Change Ltd., *The Rising Price of Love,* Hodder, London, 1995, <www.globalchange.com>.

ANNUAL HEALTH CARE COSTS
UK: Patrick Dixon *op cit*

USA: Janice Hopkins Tanne, "News: US has epidemic of sexually-transmitted disease," *British Medical Journal*, December 12, 1998, 317, p 1616.

MARRIAGE AND DIVORCE
Patrick Dixon, *op cit*

David Blanchflower and Andrew Oswald, "SOCIETY. Happy marriage 'worth HK$777,000,'" *South China Morning Post*, November 17, 1999, p 15.

LIVING TOGETHER
Jon Henley, "International News: French right up in arms over new law," *The Guardian Weekly* vol. 159 issue 20, week ending November 15, 1998, p 3.

PROSTITUTION
Donna M. Hughes, "The Internet and the Global Prostitution Industry," The Coalition Against Trafficking in Women, <www.uri.edu/artsci/wms/hughes/catw>, 1999

Australia: Alan Merridew, "Toronto tries to keep hookers in their place," *South China Morning Post*, July 8, 1995, p 19.
Indonesia: ILO 1998

Taiwan: "Taiwanese 'pay HK$17b for sex'," *Hong Kong Standard*, June 23, 1996, p 8.

Indonesia and Thailand: ILO 1998

Tuvalu: "Sex line bonanza," *South China Morning Post*, February 19, 1997, p 11

SEX CRIME
US Victim Costs and Consequences: A New Look. Series: NIJ Research Report, National Institute of Justice, January 1996 <www.ojp.usdoj.gov/>

HOMOSEXUALITY
Rachel Bridge, "Gay festival spells big business," *Sunday Morning Post*, March 3, 1996, p 4.

PORNOGRAPHY
Marty Rimm, "Marketing Pornography on the Information Superhighway: A Survey of 917,410 Images, Description, Short Stories and Animations Downloaded 8.5 Million Times by Consumers in Over 2000 Cities in Forty Countries, Provinces and Territories," *Georgetown Law Journal*, Volume 83, Issue 5, 1995.

Gareth Sansom, "Illegal and offensive content on the information highway, A Background Paper," *Long Range Planning & Analysis* (DPP), Spectrum, Information Technologies and Telecommunications Sector (SITT) Industry, Electronic Frontier Canada. Aussi disponible en français sous le titre: Le Contenu illégal et offensant sur l'autoroute de l'information. June 19, 1995 <www.efc.ca/pages/doc/offensive.html>

Report of the Attorney General's Task Force on Family Violence, U.S. Department of Justice, Washington, D.C., 112, in Richard D. Land, "Pornography and the Internet," *Light*, March–April, 1997.

Kerby Anderson, "Probe Ministries: The Pornography Plague," Telling the Truth Project from *Washington Post* web site

"The Documented Effects of Pornography 11/90," The Forerunner site via *Washington Post*. 8 Nov 1999: downloaded.

Christopher Goodwin, "Porn HK$77b-a-year industry," *The Sunday Times in Los Angeles* in *South China Morning Post*, September 7, 1998, p 14.

Donna M. Hughes *op cit*

SAFER SEX
Proposed Merger Agreed with Seton Scholl/Continued Earnings Growth at LIG, 24th May 1999. <www.durex.com>

SEX ENHANCEMENT
Merryl Lynch Viagra forecast, 1999. <www.globalchange.com>

64-65 PORNOGRAPHY

SEX ONLINE
The European, April 14–20, 1995.

Japan: "JAPAN: Child pornography capital to toughen laws on Lolita trade," Interpol report in *The Guardian* in Tokyo, in *South China Morning Post*, April 28, 1999, p 10.

ATTITUDES TO PORNOGRAPHY
Osmo Kontula and Elina Haavio-Mannila, *Sexual Pleasures: Enhancement of Sex Life in Finland*, 1971-1992, Dartmouth

SHOPPING FOR SEX
Robert T Michael, John H Gagnon, Edward O Laumann, Gina Kolata, "Table 14: Percent purchasing autoerotic materials in the past 12 months," in *Sex in America: A definitive survey*, (National Health and Social Life Survey, NHSLS 1992). Little, Brown and Co., 1994, p 157

TV SEX
"Playboy announces 1999 first quarter results," Playboy Enterprises, Inc, May 4, 1999: <www.playboy.com>

PLAYBOY
Playboy Enterprises, Inc. Fact Sheet, 1999 <www.playboy.com>

USA (right): Brian Steinberg, "Playboy Goes To School To Replenish Magazine Readership," (*Cassandra Report*, July 1999) in *The Wall Street Journal Interactive Edition*, July 16, 1999.

USA (left): Kerby Anderson, "The Pornography Plague," *Washington Post* website, downloaded November 8, 1999.

ONLINE CENSORSHIP
Mike Perry, SURVEY.NET Poll Results – Sex Survey #1, 1995-1999 Inter Commerce Corporation, <www.survey.net>

COMMENTARY ON THE MAPS
Stephen Gould, "The production, marketing, and consumption of sexually explicit materials," *Journal of Public Policy & Marketing*, 1992, vol.11, p 135. <ww2.svc.ctc.edu/dept/Psychology/psych117/pornogra2.htm>

Avedon Carol, "The Harm of Porn: Just Another Excuse to Censor, *Feminists against Censorship* 1999. <www.fiawol.demon.co.uk/FAC>

Press Release: Cyber-Rights & Cyber-Liberties (UK), Memorandum for the Internet Content Summit 1999, A Bertelsmann Foundation Conference, Munich, Germany, September 9-11, 1999. <www.cyber-rights.org>

Howard Schneider in Toronto, "Court rules bare breasts are legal," *Guardian Weekly*, December 22, 1996, p 12.

Murray Campbell in Toronto, "Debate on porn inflames nation," *South China Morning Post*, April 30, 1999.

"A storm in a 36-D cup," *South China Morning Post*, June 21, 1997, p 21.

"Chip off the old block left uncut," *South China Morning Post*, August 2, 1995, p 3.

Nick Cater, "India's tentative sexual revolution," *South China Morning Post*, June 18, 1996, p 17.

Zahid Hussain in Karachi, "Tom and Jerry among zealous censors' victims," *South China Morning Post*, November 10, 1999, p 13.

Alexandra Frean, "Our audience is worried about standards: BBC to take a new look at taste and decency," *The Times*, July 5 1995, p 9.

David Brake, "FORUM: Surfing with the blinkers on," *New Scientist*, September 20, 1997.

Cass R. Sunstein, "Pornography and the First Amendment," *Duke Law Journal,* September 1986, pp 595ff.

Robert T. Franceour, *The International Encyclopedia of Sexuality*, Continuum, New York, 1999.

66-67 PROSTITUTION

LEGAL STATUS
Robert T. Franceour, *The International Encyclopedia of Sexuality*, Continuum, New York, 1999.

The World Sex Guide, 1999 <www.worldsexguide.org>

USA (left): "Kerb crawlers sent to the classroom," *South China Morning Post*, March 29, 1997, p 5.

USA (right): Tom W. Smith, *American Sexual Behavior: Trends, Socio-Demographic Differences, and Risk Behavior*, National Opinion Research Center, University of Chicago, *GSS Topical Report* no. 25, December, 1994.

Asia: Elif Kaban, "UN body urges governments to recognise sex trade," International Labour Organization, ILO, Reuters, Geneva, August 19, 1998.

CHILD PROSTITUTES
UNICEF, 1999

ECPAT (End Child Prostitution in Asian Tourism), World Congress Against Commercial Sexual Exploitation of Children (Thailand), 1994. <www.epcat.org>

FREQUENCY OF PURCHASING SEX
J. Lowman, C. Atchison, and L. Fraser, "Men Who Buy Sex, Phase 2: The Client Survey, Preliminary Findings" internet survey, 1997. <users.uniserve.com/~lowman/ICSS/icss.htm>

THE PICK-UP
J. Lowman *op cit*

INTERNATIONAL MIGRATION OF FEMALE PROSTITUTES
(IOM) International Organization for Migration, 1998 various internet sites, including,
Migrant Women from Central and Eastern Europe (IOM)
</www.iom.int:9798/doc/MIP_TRAFWMN.htm>

Sex Industry in Southeast Asia (ILO-Report)
<www.ilo.org/public/english/235press/pr/1998/31.htm>

Trafficking in Women from the Dominican Republic (IOM)
<www.iom.int:9798/doc/MIP_Dominica.ht>

Trafficking in Women to Austria (IOM)
<www.iom.int:9798/doc/MIP_Austria.htm>

Trafficking in Women to Italy (IOM)
<www.iom.int:9798/doc/MIP_Italy.ht>

Trafficking of Cambodian women and children to Thailand (IOM)
<www.iom.int:9798/publications/Publications_Survey_and_studie s/Cambodia/Cam_1.html>

SEX ACTS MOST FREQUENTLY PURCHASED
J. Lowman *op cit*

Amy Chouinard and Jacques Albert, eds., *Human Sexuality: Research Perspectives in a world facing AIDS*, IDRC Workshop, Canada, June 1989,

COMMENTARY ON THE MAPS
World Charter For Prostitutes' Rights
<www.bayswan.org/ICPRChart./html>

68-69 SEX TOURISM

INTERNATIONAL SEX TOURISTS
ECPAT (End Child Prostitution in Asian Tourism), World Congress Against Commercial Sexual Exploitation of Children, 1994.
<www.ecpat.org>

ARRESTS IN ASIA
United States National Center for Missing and Exploited Children, cited in UNICEF's "Breaking the walls of silence a UNICEF background paper on the sexual exploitation of children," July 1994.

Ron O'Grady, "The rape of the innocent," ECPAT (End Child Prostitution in Asian Tourism), World Congress Against Commercial Sexual Exploitation of Children (Thailand), 1994.
<www.ecpat.org>

COMMENTARY ON THE MAPS
ECPAT (End Child Prostitution in Asian Tourism) *op cit*

Martin Staebler, "Tourism and children in prostitution," working document for the World Congress against Commercial Sexual Exploitation of Children 1994, <www.epcat.org>

Part Six SEXUAL RITES

72-73 RELIGION

RELIGIONS OF THE WORLD
Joanne O'Brien and Martin Palmer, *The State of Religion Atlas*, Simon & Schuster, London and New York, 1993, pp 16-17.

OFFICAL POSITIONS
Ontario Consultants on Religious Tolerance
<www.religioustolerance.org>

Farooq Nasim Bhutti, "Effect of religion (Islam) and pro-western culture on incidence of early ejaculation and treatment most suitable in conservative Muslim society like Pakistan," 14th World Congress of Sexology, Hong Kong, August 23–27, 1999, Abstract book p 294.

Paul Sachdev, "Sexual evolution or Sexual revolution: A study of attitudes and behaviors among University Students in Delhi, India," 14th World Congress of Sexology, Hong Kong; August 23–27 1999, Abstract book p 108.

Robert T. Franceour, *The International Encyclopedia of Sexuality.* Continuum, New York, 1999, p 585.

World Legal Survey, The International Lesbian and Gay Association (ILGA), 2000, <www.ilga.org>

Tinja Tsang, "Consumer guide to religion," *Sunday Morning Post Magazine*, February 25, 1996, pp 9–11.

PROTESTANTS' VIEWS ON ADULTERY
Katherine Towers, "Protestants oppose sex outside wedlock,"
The Australian, February 15, 1995, p 5.

RELIGION AND SEXUAL ORIENTATION
The National Coalition for Gay, Lesbian, Bisexual and
Transgender Youth and Oasis Magazine, !OutProud!/Oasis
Internet Survey of Queer and Questioning Youth, March 1998.
<www.oasismag.com/survey/97/>

COMMENTARY ON THE MAPS
Christine Aziz, "A life of hell for the wife of a god,"
The Guardian, June 10, 1995.

Christopher Thomas, "Handmaidens in a cult become priests'
sexual property," *South China Morning Post*, January 24, 1997,
p 14.

Christine Aziz, "Where priests keep children as sex slaves,"
Marie Claire, August 1966, pp 92–96.

"Wedding unites thousands of strangers," *South China Morning
Post*, February 14, 2000, p 8.

Owen Boycott, "Church denies gay man has right to be
godfather," *Weekly Guardian*, August 20, 1995, p 11.

"Wedding ban," *Sunday Morning Post*, March 31, 1996, p 8.

The National Coalition for Gay, Lesbian, Bisexual and
Transgender Youth and Oasis Magazine, !OutProud!/Oasis, *op cit*

74-75 FEMALE GENITAL EXCISION

FEMALE GENITAL EXCISION
WHO Technical Working Group on Female Genital Mutilation,
Geneva, July 17–19, 1995, and Joint WHO/UNFPA/UNICEF
statement, 1996. World Health Organization, <www.who.ch>

World Health Organization, 1999 <www.who.ch>

Population Action International, Washington DC, USA, 1999

UK: Rupert Walder, IPPF, "Why the problem (female genital
mutilation) continues in Britain," *British Medical Journal*
May 20, 1995; 6990:310, pp 1593–94.

France: Colette Gallard, "Female genital mutilation in France,"
British Medical Journal, May 20, 1995; 6990:310, pp 1592–93.

USA: Norra Macready, "Female genital mutilation outlawed in
US," *British Medical Journal*, November 2, 1996, 313, p 1103.

Wanda Jones, Jack Smith, Burney Kieke, Lynne Wilcox, "Female
Genital Mutilation/Female Circumcision," *Public Health Reports,*
September/October 1997, Vol 112, pp 368–377.

INCREASE IN FGE
Reuter, "UN calls for end to sexual mutilation," *The Guardian
Weekly*, Volume 156, Issue 16 for week ending April 20, 1997,
p 7.

COMMENTARY ON THE MAPS
WHO Technical Working Group on Female Genital Mutilation,
op cit

F. Hosken, *The Hosken report on genital and sexual mutilation of
females*, Women's International Network News, 1982.

J. A. Black and G. D. Debelle, "Female genital mutilation in
Britain," *British Medical Journal*, June 17, 1995; 310,
pp 1590–94.

"A traditional practice that threatens health – female
circumcision," *WHO Chronicle*, 40 (1): 31–36 (1986), p 33

Dr Hassan Y. Aboul-Enein, Saudi Arabia, letter to the Editor,
WHO World Health Forum. 8 (1)(1987), p 241.

Hamid Rushwan, "Female circumcision," *World Health,*
April–May 1990, pp 24–25.

Josh Hamilton, "UN condemns female circumcision," *British
Medical Journal*, April 19, 1997, (324), p 1148.

76-77 CIRCUMCISION

CIRCUMCISED MEN
Joanne O'Brien and Martin Palmer, *The State of Religion Atlas*.
Simon & Schuster, London and New York, 1993.

National Organisation to Halt the Abuse and Routine Mutilation
of Males (HOHARMM), 1999

TRENDS IN CIRCUMCISION
The National Center for Health Statistics of the Department of
Heath and Human Services, U.S. Federal Government

DISTRIBUTION OF CIRCUMCISED MEN WORLDWIDE
"Total Estimated Number of Circumcised Males Now Living
(Muslim, Jewish, North American, and African Tribal populations
only)," in *Estimated Worldwide Incidence of Male Circumcision
Complications*, National Organisation to Halt the Abuse and
Routine Mutilation of Males (NOHARMM), May 29, 1999.

CUT RATE
The National Center for Health Statistics, Department of Health
and Human Services, USA.

"Awakenings" A Preliminary Poll of Circumcised Men, National
Organisation to Halt the Abuse and Routine Mutilation of Males
(NOHARMM), March 1996. <www.noharmm.org>

Circumcision FactFinder: Research Page for the News Media,
Statistics at National Organisation to Halt the Abuse and Routine
Mutilation of Males (NOHARMM), May 29, 1999.
<www.noharmm.org/factfinder.htm>

COMMENTARY ON THE MAPS
"Circumcision: A Medical or a Human Rights Issue?" *Journal of
Nurse-Midwifery* vol. 37, no. 2 Supplement, March/April 1992.

Van Howe, "Circumcision and HIV infection: review of the
literature and meta-analysis," *Internation Journal of STD and
AIDS,* January 1999, 10(1), pp 8–16.

Stephen Moses, Robert C Bailey, Allan R Ronald, "Male
circumcision: assessment of health benefits and risks," *Sexually
Transmitted Infections* 1998; 74, pp 368–373

Regional Center of the National Organization of Circumcision
Information Resource Centers, NOCIRC, Seattle, Washington, US,
1999. Via <www.noharmm.org>

Robert S. Thompson, "Routine Circumcision in the Newborn: An
Opposing View," *Journal of Family Practice*, 1990, vol. 31, no. 2,
pp 189–96.

Part Seven SEX CRIMES

80-81 SEXUAL HARASSMENT

LEGISLATION
The National Anti-Stalking and Harassment Support Association (NASH), 1999.

Australia: Rachel Bridge, AFP, "Sex harassment pervades Navy," *South China Morning Post*, November 3, 1997, p 15.

Japan: 1996 Human Rights Report: Japan <www.state.gov/www/global/human_rights/1996_hrp_report/japan.html>

Mexico: R. Carrillo, "Battered dreams. Gender violence and development," *POPULI*, November 1992;19(5), pp 7–9.

Taiwan: Tang Tzu-chun, "Psychosomatic symptoms from sexual harassment experiences of one nursing college in Southern Taiwan," 14th World Congress of Sexology, Hong Kong, August 23–27 1999, Abstract book p 282.

UK and USA: "A glaring ommission," *Cosmopolitan*, April 1995, p 79.

USA: Karin Bishop,"Campus sex pest problem," *South China Morning Post*, November 19, 1994, p 6.

USA and Canada: K.M. Abrams and G.E. Robinson,"Stalking. Part I: An overview of the problem," *Canadian Journal of Psychiatry*, June 1998;43(5), pp 473–76.

INCREASE IN SEXUAL HARASSMENT CASES
Mark Hansen, "Number of sexual harassment claims filed with the Commission and similar state agencies, USA federal Equal Opportunities Commission," *ABA Journal* September 1998, p 28.

Federal Equal Employment Opportunity Commission (EEOC), reported by John Cloud, "Sex and the law," *Time*, March 23, 1998, pp 22–28.

SEXUAL HARASSMENT OF WOMEN AT WORK
University of Manchester Institute of Science and Technology, 1995, in "Handling harassment," *Cosmopolitan* April 1995, p 102.

Kyodo in Tokyo, "One in six state staff face sex demands," National Personnel Authority survey, in *South China Morning Post*, March 12, 1998, p 14.

AFP in Tokyo, "Sex pests are rampant," *South China Morning Post*, March 1, 1998, p B3.

HOMOPHOBIC HARASSMENT AT SCHOOL
The National Coalition for Gay, Lesbian, Bisexual and Transgender Youth and Oasis Magazine, !OutProud!/Oasis Internet Survey of Queer and Questioning Youth, March 1998. <www.oasismag.com/survey/97/>

CYBER-HARASSMENT
Stephanie Armour, "Offensive e-mail in office on increase," *USA Today*, April 5, 1999

"More Than 1 Million Women Harassed Online," APBnews.com, September 30, 1999.

"A Special News Report About Life On the Job – and Trends Taking Shape There: Companies Crack Down on the Increasing Sexual Harassment by E-Mail," MI Press Clip, September 22, 1999 <www.elronsoftware.com>

COMMENTARY ON THE MAPS
Joseph S. Fulda, "The Complexities of Sexual Harassment: A Sociobiological Perspective (1)", November 30, 1999.

John Cloud, "Sex and the law," *Time*, March 23, 1998, pp 22–28.

Marcel Berlins, "The stalker and the stalked," *Law in Action*, BBC Radio 4, in Virgin Issues, HotAir, April to June 1996, p 15.

Linda Grant, "The slow torture of being stalked," *Cosmopolitan*, April 1995, pp 13–16.

National Victim Center in Washington D.C., USA, 1999. <www.nvc.org>

82-83 SEXUAL VIOLENCE

FEMALE RAPE
UNDP (United Nations Development Programme), Human Development Indicators, *Human Development Report* 1999. Table 23: Crime.

Lynne Duke, "Child rape reaches epidemic scale," *Washington Post*, in *Guardian Weekly*, March 7, 1997, p 17.

"No deterrent," *South China Morning Post*, October 18, 1999, p 10.

Abortion Laws Worldwide, Population Action International, 1993.

Australia: John Slee, Legal Correspondent, "One in 4 Prisoners Sexually Assaulted," *Sydney Morning Herald*, September 24, 1996, p 9.

France: Public Prosecutor at the Court of Appeal of Lyon, September 5, 1990. *Semaine Juridique.* 1991; (6):Jurisprudence pp 38–41.

Spain: H. Martinez-Ayala *et al* "[Sexual aggression in adolescents. Epidemiologic study]"[Article in Spanish], *Ginecol Obstet Mex,* September 1999 67, pp 449–53.

UK: Adrian Coxell, Michael King, Gillian Mezey, Dawn Gordon, "General Practice: Lifetime prevalence, characteristics, and associated problems of non-consensual sex in men: cross sectional survey," *British Medical Journal*, March 27, 1999; 318, pp 846–50.

USA: *The Barnard/Columbia Women's Handbook* 1992, chapter 8: <www.gopher.cc.columbia.edu.71/00/publications/women/wh52> 30 Nov 1999: downloaded

REOFFENDERS
P. Firestone *et al.* "Recidivism in convicted rapists," *Journal American Academy of Psychiatry Law* 1998, 26(2), pp 185–200.

CHILD SEX ABUSE
P. Bouvier *et al.* "Typology and correlates of sexual abuse in children and youth: multivariate analyses in a prevalence study in Geneva," *Child Abuse Neglect* August 1999, 23 (8), pp 779–90.

ABUSERS
Martin Wong, "Third of students 'sex abuse victims,'" *South China Morning Post*, November 10, 1999.

MALE RAPE
M. King and E. Woollett, "Sexually assaulted males: 115 men consulting a counselling service," *Archive of Sexual Behavior*, December 1997, 26(6), pp 579–88.

COMMENTARY ON THE MAPS

W P de Silva, "Clinical review: ABC of sexual health – Sexual variations," *British Medical Journal*, March 6, 1999; 318, pp 654–56.

Michael Ellison, "The men can't help it," *The Guardian*, January 25, 2000, p 4.

Barry Hugill, "Paedophilia is not the preserve of a few sick individuals. It's a billion dollar business," *The Observer*, August 25, 1996, p 19.

David Connett and Jon Henley, "The Child Abusers: These men are not paedophiles: they are Internet abusers," *The Observer*, August 25, 1996, p 19.

V. I. Rickert and C.M. Wiemann, "Date rape among adolescents and young adults," *Journal of Pediatric Adolescent Gynecology*, 11(4), November 1998, pp 167–75.

P.Y. Symons *et al*, "Prevalence and predictors of adolescent dating violence," *Journal of Child Adolescent Psychiatry Nursing*, 7(3), July–September 1994, pp 14–23.

A. Cohall *et al*, "Love shouldn't hurt: strategies for health care providers to address adolescent dating violence," *Journal of the American Womens Association,* Summer 1999 54(3), pp 144–48.

Part Eight EVOLUTIONS

86-87 THE FUTURE OF SEX

Eli Coleman, "Revolutionary Changes in Sexuality in the new Millennium: Sexual health, diversity and sexual rights," University of Minnesota, USA. 14th World Congress of Sexology, Hong Kong; August 23-27, 1999, Abstract book p 33.

Matt Ridley, "Visions of the 21st Century: Will We Still Need to Have Sex?" *Time*, November 1, 1999.

Ian Pearson, *The Macmillan Atlas of the Future* Macmillan, New York, 1998; *The Atlas of the Future*, Routledge, London, 1998.

Part Nine TABLES

90-91 CHRONOLOGY OF HUMAN SEXUAL BEHAVIOR

T. Taylor, *The Prehistory of Sex*, Fourth Estate, London, 1996.

Robert Koch Institute, Berlin, Germany, Archiv für Sexualwissenschaft/Archive for Sexology, III. *Modern Sex Research* (1938 –), 2000. <www.rki.ge/GESUND/ARCHIV/HOME.HTM>

Eli Coleman, "Revolutionary Changes in Sexuality in the new Millennium: Sexual health, diversity and sexual rights," University of Minnesota, USA. 14th World Congress of Sexology, Hong Kong; August 23-27, 1999, Abstract book p 33.

92-93 APHRODISIACS

Charles Henry Connell, *Aphrodisiacs in your Garden*, Arthur Barker, 1966.

Alan Hull Walton, *Aphrodisiacs from legend to prescription. A Study of Aphrodisiacs through the Ages*, London, 1958.

Harry Ezekiel Wedeck, *Dictionary of Aphrodisiacs*, Peter Owen, London, 1962.

SELECT BIBLIOGRAPHY

Alan Guttmacher Institute, *Into A New World: Young Women's Sexual and Reproductive Lives, 1998.* <agi-usa.org/home.html>

ASPRS (American Society of Plastic and Reconstructive Surgeons), <www.plasticsurgery.org/>

BBC World Service Education (BBC) and International Planned Parenthood Federation (IPPF), "Sexwise," 1999 <www.bbc.co.uk/worldservice/sexwise>

Benewick Robert, and Stephanie Donald, *The State of China Atlas,* Penguin, London and New York, 1999

CDC (Centers for Disease Control and Prevention), USA: Health Topics A to Z. <cdc.gov/health/diseases.htm.>

CIRP (Circumcision Information Resource Pages) <www.cirp.org/>

Coleman Eli, "Revolutionary Changes in Sexuality in the new Millennium: Sexual health, diversity and sexual rights," University of Minnesota, USA. 14th World Congress of Sexology, Hong Kong; August 23–27, 1999, Abstract book p 33

Demographic and Health Surveys and Knowledge, Attitudes, Beliefs and Practices Surveys, annual. <www.macroint.com/dhs>

Dotlove: Chinese language youth internet web site on love, relationships and sex. <www.dotlove.com>

Durex Global Sex Surveys, 1996, 1997, 1998, 1999 <www.durex.com/>, <www.durex.com/scientific/>

ECPAT (End Child Prostitution in Asian Tourism), <www.epcat.org>

Francoeur, Robert T., *The International Encyclopedia of Sexuality. Continuum,* New York, 1999

Global Change Ltd <www.globalchange.com>

IGLA (International Lesbian and Gay Association), <www.ilga.org>

IPPF (International Planned Parenthood Federation). <www.ippf.org/index.htm>

Kama Sutra, translated by Indra Sinha, Spring Books, 1980.

Kinsey Institute for Research in Sex, Gender, and Reproduction, Inc. <www.indiana.edu/~kinsey/>

Lowman, J. Atchison, C. and Fraser, L. "Men Who Buy Sex, Phase 2: The Client Survey, Preliminary Findings", 1997. <users.uniserve.com/~lowman/ICSS/icss.htm>

Michael, Robert T, John H Gagnon, Edward O Laumann, Gina Kolata, "Sex in America: A definitive survey," *National Health and Social Life Survey,* NHSLS 1992. Little, Brown and Co., 1994.

National Coalition for Gay, Lesbian, Bisexual and Transgender Youth and Oasis Magazine,"!OutProud!/Oasis Internet Survey of Queer and Questioning Youth, USA. <www.oasismag.com/>

National Victim Center, Washington D.C, USA <www.nvc.org>

NISSO: Netherlands Institute for Social and Sexological Research. <www.niwi.knaw.nl/guests/nisso/>

NOHARMM (National Organisation to Halt the Abuse and Routine Mutilation of Males) <www.noharmm.org/>

O'Brien, Joanne and Martin Palmer, *The State of Religion Atlas*, Simon and Schuster, London and New York, 1993

Ontario Consultants on Religious Tolerance <www.religioustolerance.org/>

Pearson, Ian, *The Macmillan Atlas of the Future* Macmillan, New York; *The Atlas of the Future*, Routledge, London, 1998.

Population Action International, <www.populationaction.org/>

POPINFORM, POPLINE and Population Reports, Population Information Program, Center for Communication Programs, Johns Hopkins University School of Public Health, USA.

POPINFORM: <db.jhuccp.org/popinform/index.stm>

POPLINE: <www.jhuccp.org/popline/index.stm>

Ridley, Matt, *The Red Queen: Sex and the Evolution of Human Nature*, Penguin, London, 1994

Robert Koch Institute, Berlin, Germany, Archive of Sexology. <www.rki.ge/GESUND/ARCHIV/HOME.HTM>

Seager, Joni, *The State of Women in the World Atlas*, Penguin, London and New York, 1997.

SIECUS: Sexuality Information and Education Council of the United States. <www.siecus.org/>

Smith, Anthony, *The Human Body*, BBC Books, London, 1998.

Smith, Tom W., *American Sexual Behavior: Trends, Socio-Demographic Differences, and Risk Behavior,* National Opinion Research Center, University of Chicago, GSS Topical Report No. 25, December, 1994. <www.icpsr.umich.edu/gss/report/t-report/topic25.htm>

SURVEY.NET Poll Results – Sex Survey #1, 1995–1999 Inter Commerce Corporation. <www.survey.net/>

UN Statistical Databases <www.un.org.pk/StatData.html>

UNAIDS, *AIDS Epidemic Update*: December 1999, UNAIDS, Geneva <www.unaids.org>

UNDP *Human Development Report* 1999 <www.undp.org/hdro/>

UNFPA (United Nations Population Fund) <www.unfpa.org/>

US Bureau of the Census, International Data Base (IDB) <www.census.gov/ftp/pub/ipc/www/idbnew.html>

Victim Service Programs <www.vaonline.org/vsu.html>

Wellings, Kate, Julia Field, Anne M. Johnson, Jane Wadsworth, *Sexual Behaviour in Britain: The National Survey of Sexual Attitudes and Lifestyles*, Penguin, London, 1994.

Westheimer, Ruth, *Dr Ruth's Encyclopedia of Sex*, Continuum, New York, 1994.

WHO (World Health Organization) <www.who.ch>

INDEX